The
PLAYBOY
GUIDE
to
BACHELOR
PARTIES

Everything You Need to Know About
Planning the Groom's Rite of Passage—

FROM SIMPLE TO
Sinful

JAMES OLIVER CURY

A Fireside Book

NEW YORK LONDON TORONTO SYDNEY SINGAPORE

FIRESIDE
Rockefeller Center
1230 Avenue of the Americas
New York, NY 10020

For information about special discounts for bulk purchases,
please contact Simon & Schuster Special Sales:
1-800-456-6798 or business@simonandschuster.com

Designed by Joy O'Meara-Battista

Manufactured in the United States of America

1   3   5   7   9   10   8   6   4   2

Library of Congress Cataloging-in-Publication Data is available.

ISBN 0-7432-3289-5

CONTENTS

FOUR

Hot Spots: Las Vegas, Tijuana, and New Orleans

FIVE

Beyond the Bachelor Party

The
PLAYBOY
GUIDE
to
BACHELOR
PARTIES

ONE
Planning Basics

Introduction

There are two types of bachelor parties.

The first is the traditional, stereotypical, female-form-fetish-izing, push-the-limits fest and includes any or all of the following: booze, porno films, strippers, escorts, gambling, drinking games, and sworn secrecy. You can experience any combination of these diversions in a hotel, strip club, or bar. I refer to this is an R-rated party.

The second type of bachelor party—growing in popularity—rejects the depravity. There are no crazy moments where piss-drunk Pete wears a dildo on his head and uses it on the hired help. Instead, a bunch of friends spend an evening or whole weekend bonding in the midst of more benign activities. This is a PG-rated party.

Within the latter group, there are three categories: outdoorsy/athletic, swanky, and inexpensive. These include baseball games, fishing trips, boat parties, golfing jaunts, laser tag/paintball excursions, camping trips, extreme sports, billiards nights, poker games, barbecues, arcade nights, wine tastings, gambling, and many other activities. This night won't likely become the stuff of legend, but it also won't make anyone blush or wince in retrospect.

What's interesting is that the men who advocate an R-rated

trivia: Stag parties aren't just a modern-day event. They were first held by ancient Spartan soldiers, who partied like it was 999. The first known such party took place in the fifth century. Members of the military celebrated with a feast and toast to the groom on the eve of his wedding. This was a way to reminisce about the past, mourn the death of the bachelor status, and raise money for the groom so he could continue to drink with his friends after his wife got control of the finances.

bachelor party can't imagine why anyone would want to just play a wimpy game of golf or have a steak dinner when they could see naked chicks on the one night you're expected to do so. And the men who want a more refined bachelor party do not understand why men would subject themselves to a night of sexual frustration, paying hundreds of dollars to see women they don't know tease them.

But guess what? There's no reason why a party can't schedule innocent fun by day and lascivious fun by night. The point is: No matter what the groom likes, there is an ideal party for him just waiting to happen. And no matter how ribald or tame, this book can help you plan it.

What Usually Goes Wrong—and Why

Planning a bachelor party is relatively easy. The problem is that few men recognize that they have to be planned. Guys assume that all they need is $100 in their pocket. Then, after a hearty steak meal, the group of twelve buddies congregates on the corner outside wondering who's supposed to lead (the groom or the best man or the dude who knows the local strip clubs?).

This is exactly what happened at a bachelor party I once attended. We left the steakhouse as a group and waffled outside for twenty minutes until some of us started to get restless. Since there was no plan in advance, some guys decided to leave immediately. The remaining guys bickered about where to go; I felt like I was watching an exercise in leadership training. Do we go to a bar? Disco? Strip club? Or home for the night?

We ended up visiting strippers in midtown Manhattan, but none of us had any idea how much it would cost, how much to tip, or how to fend off the overly aggressive strippers who relentlessly prodded us for more $20 lap dances (plus tips). Nor did we come equipped with single-dollar bills. Very few of the guys really wanted the night to end this way. It just seemed like the only option. It wasn't and we should have known better.

One solution is to plan at least three or four different activities or events throughout the evening. This gives people time to duck out early or enter late. You might also include a battle plan that goes into the wee hours for those who survive that long—with or without the groom. (See the chart at the end of this book for an at-a-glance, mix and-match look at *all* of the activities described in this book.)

Too many activities, however, can lead to other problems—like premature drunkenness and/or fatigue. At another bachelor party I attended, fifteen of my friends had assembled in a hotel room and started to drink while they waited for the entertainment to arrive. By the time the two strippers showed up, the groom had drunk himself senseless and thrown up in the bathroom (where the strippers were supposed to change into costume).

Worse, if possible, was the dynamic in the room: the men were scared. These guys were not rah-rah types and the sight of two (admittedly skanky) strippers made otherwise confident men very nervous. The guys hid in corners, pretending to be deep in intellectual conversation or fixing more drinks—anything to avoid the discomfort of watching these women get jiggy.

It wasn't just awkward for the party attendees either; strippers crave the spotlight and love enthusiastic crowds. They want the men to go crazy when they enter a room—they have to pump their egos and they rely on tips to make money. Regardless of whether it was shyness, revulsion, or political correctness, the men's behavior made the strippers wonder what was wrong. That's a bad way to start a wild night. Having strippers was not a bad idea. But the best man should have monitored the groom's drinking and made sure the crowd knew what it was getting. Planning is everything.

BACHELOR PARTY PEER PRESSURE

No matter how sophisticated, mild-mannered, educated, or sweet the groom may be, there will be pressure for the best man to plan a raucous bachelor party. Inevitably, one of his buddies will want strippers, and he'll make it known that it's not "really" a bachelor party without gratuitous nudity. He is wrong. Do not pander to the suggestions of a macho moron—unless he's the groom.

trivia: The world's most famous bachelor pad—the Playboy Mansion—has never hosted a bachelor party . . . even for Mr. Hefner himself.

Strippers are fine for some guys, but not for others. Some men wouldn't consider a bachelor party without babes and booze. That's the norm and this book explains what you need to know so the adult entertainment business doesn't disappoint or scam you. But it's important to consider the alternatives, too. Sometimes, all a party needs is a blow-up doll and some chocolate, boob-shaped lollipops to meet the minimum, wink-wink-nudge-nudge bachelor party requirements. To you I say: There, you've been naughty. Now you can move on to something creative.

Who, When, Where?

WHO PLANS IT?

There's a reason why he's called the best man. And here's his opportunity to live up to the title. It's up to this one guy to discuss party options with either the groom or the other invitees (depending on whether the party is naughty or not) and subsequently create an itinerary for the night or weekend. The best man is usually the groom's brother or best friend.

If the best man is not going to attend the bachelor party, for whatever the reason, dig up a substitute.

BEST MAN'S RESPONSIBILITIES

The best man orders and pays—often in advance—for a hotel room, limo, stripper, bar, restaurant, booze, tickets for shows, and any other service that requires a deposit. He not only tells the gang what's happening, but where it will be, when, and how much everyone must chip in. Then, he'll have to keep track of who has RSVP'd and later, it will be his job to collect the cash before or during the party (never wait until it's over). The *best* best man knows exactly what the groom does *and doesn't* want. If there's any doubt, he should consult the groom. The party will have enough surprises.

PAYMENT

A best man rarely collects every cent from every member of the party. He needs to recruit a few fellow bachelor party attendees to put up cash in advance as needed. The best man should also delegate the collection of money from the rest of the party attendees. To do this, he must ask some friends to collect from others and to keep track of who's paid.

Don't do it alone; you will pay more than your share and likely wind up angry. Better to overestimate the per-person costs. No one minds getting cash back after the party, but they will all groan if you tell them that they owe money.

If you're the best man, think of the money-gathering process as selling a script. You have to come up with the pitch, paint the picture, and then get financial backers.

Here's a checklist to get you started:

- Find out how many people will attend—and who they are.
- Find out what the groom likes and doesn't like—R-rated party or not.
- Find out what the attendees are willing to pay (make it sound unbelievably fun to get more cash).

tip: Consider using an on-line payment program, like Paypal, to collect contributions from fellow bachelor party attendees. That way you can track who paid, when they paid, and cash never needs to pass hands.

tip: Pad your estimate when asking for money from the bachelor party attendees. This will cover unexpected fees and, if there's a surplus, you can always dole out singles to the guys for later use when tipping the girls.

- Call around or do on-line research to get a ballpark idea of costs.
- Get the money from the guys in advance, if possible.
- Keep written records of who has paid and *when* they paid.

10 Things the Best Man Should Bring to the Party

1. List of all attendees
2. Attendees' phone numbers
3. Taxi company phone numbers
4. Cell phone
5. Bottle opener
6. Mints
7. Extra cash (for gratuities and emergencies)
8. Credit cards (for hotel rooms, bar tabs, emergencies)
9. The evening's itinerary
10. Aspirin

WHEN TO PLAN IT

Timing is key. Too much and everything changes; people move, forget, or make other plans. Too little time and you're left with one option: local restaurants, billiard halls, bowling alleys, pool halls,

tip: You can ask the groom what kind of party he would like and still not ruin some of the surprise of the evening. You wouldn't want those dancing naked midgets to go unappreciated.

bars, and so on—assuming you can get in, late at night, with a group, on a Friday or Saturday.

First, you need to know when the wedding will take place. Then, find out if the groom has a bachelor-party date in mind. Two months to plan the event is best. Four weeks is as short as it should get. Remember, this is when to plan it—not when to have it.

The earlier you establish an itinerary, the better. This helps invitees mark it on their schedules before other events conflict and it allows out-of-town guests to book flights and hotel rooms. It also helps you get reservations at restaurants, clubs, golf courses, ski lodges, white-water rafting companies, etc. Don't forget to secure a limo or two in advance as well. (See "Limousines 101.")

Planning Calendar

Two Months before Party
❑ Confer with groom, decide what to do, where to go, how much to spend, and who to invite.
❑ Establish budget.
❑ Delegate some of the inviting and money gathering to a few select guaranteed attendees.

Six Weeks before Party
❑ Invite all attendees and explain the details (when, where), including costs and how and when to pay.
❑ Keep a log of RSVPs.

One Month before Party
❑ Make all reservations: clubs, bars, limos, etc., based on estimated number of attendees (many will have RSVP'd by now).

Two Weeks before Party
❑ Confirm reservations with limo company, entertainers, restaurants, etc.
❑ Purchase booze, if needed.
❑ Assess RSVPs and make changes to plans as needed.

One Week before Party
❑ Have a "Plan B" ready, just in case.
❑ Assess and confirm RSVPs and make changes to plans as needed.
❑ Remind invitees that party is next week.

One Day before Party
❑ Get one- and five-dollar bills from the bank so that you can make change for the fellas.
❑ Call to confirm all reservations once again.
❑ Buy the aspirin.

Day of Party
❑ Show up at first destination 30 minutes early. Be prepared to call no-shows and later arrivals.
❑ Collect fees from all invitees if you have not done so yet.
❑ Remember to tip.

Day after Party
❑ Remind deadbeats what they owe for last night.
❑ Sleep.
❑ Explain weird hand-stamp/lipstick stains to girlfriend.
❑ Check on bachelor to make sure he is still getting married.

"Wouldn't you know it—I had the same thing for lunch."

WHEN TO HAVE IT

If this were a locals-only party, it wouldn't matter so much. But these are your old buddies, many of whom may be flying in from other cities—perhaps with family. You better make it worth their while. Your job is to plan a party that avoids crowds, last-minute reservations, and complications. At best, you'll also save your friends loads of money—which means more booze/tips/food for the party.

No one would have a bachelor party on Christmas Eve, right? So don't forget to check the calendar before planning a party on Easter, Passover, Thanksgiving, or even major holidays when people are likely to travel or vacation—like Memorial Day and Labor Day. The prices for travel and accommodations are higher on these days and your buddies may already have prior commitments.

Remember that the bride may be planning her own bachelorette party. Some couples prefer to have both parties on the same day—and then report back the following morning. Yours may be far more risqué, but this seems to level the playing field. Finally, some grooms have the bachelor party in one city and the wedding in another. This is one way to cavort with friends who live far away and cannot make it to the wedding.

tip: Arrange for the groom to stay at a friend's house on the night of the bachelor party, regardless of what is planned and what happens.

Weekend vs. Weekday

You can't host a four-day golf or camping retreat if *all* the guys have to take off a few days from work; their bosses probably won't let them go. Fridays and Saturdays are your safest bet, though most places are more crowded at this time. And you will pay more for a limo (and for reservations at hotels and spas) if you book at the busiest times. On the other hand, weekends bring out more women than do weekdays. If you do decide on a weekday, start early—6 or 7 P.M.—so you can pack in six hours of fun and still get to bed before two in the morning (most guys don't want to drink too much on a week night anyway). Ask about off-peak discounts when booking your limos, tickets to shows, and strippers. Expect to pay 20 to 30 percent less than usual.

Seasonal Advantages

Seasons affect plane fares, what you wear, and how you get around town. Ask a local hotel if there are conventions in town the weekend you want to host your party. Conventions tie up rooms and cabs and they jack up prices. Think about whether you need good weather for the party: skiing requires snow or snow machines, while boating requires mild weather. Indoor activities are more flexible. Poker, trips to Vegas, pub crawls, and Scotch tastings are ideal for the winter months. If it's a May party, for example, you might schedule a weekend at the Kentucky Derby. If it's a late summer party, consider a barbecue. And if it's in late January, you can try to score Superbowl tickets—or at least catch the game somewhere on a big screen.

Too Much Lead Time

The couple could call it off. So don't have the party months before the wedding. The more lead time, the more often someone (the best man, most likely) has to remind everyone about the event.

Make Sure There's a Firm Wedding Date

Chances are this is a given, but wedding dates sometimes change and the bachelor party must precede the wedding.

tip: Never throw a bachelor party the night before the wedding. This is an invitation for disaster. The groom may be disheveled, exhausted, embarrassed, drunk, hungover, late, or MIA. As will be the groomsmen.

The Right Answer

Anywhere from two to four weeks before the wedding is the ideal time to host a bachelor party. If the bachelor party must be scheduled closer to the wedding (perhaps friends are flying in), then make it happen at least two days before the wedding— assuming all attendees will already be in town. Also, make sure you don't schedule the bachelor party at the same time that mom and dad arranged for their out-of-towners guest dinner. The bachelor can't attend both parties on the same night.

WHERE TO HAVE IT

Usually, the city is set—it's where the groom either lives or plans to get married. If the groom is willing, the best man can plan a surprise theme in any city or state he likes. The idea is to whisk away the groom for one last weekend. This is fine unless the best man is planning a party in a city he's never visited or does not know well (hot spots include Las Vegas, New Orleans, and Tijuana). In this case, he needs to consider the following advice.

1. Gather all the relevant data: how many guys, how big a budget, and whether it's a PG- or R-rated party.
2. Contact someone who lives in the destination city. This will be your point person; he knows people who know people

who can answer *any* questions (like: What's a good-but-affordable steakhouse?).

3. If no direct contact is apparent, call someone at a business you might employ (like a bar or restaurant) and pick that person's brain. Get a second opinion. Do not trust Web sites or even books on their own. Prices change, clubs close, and reviewers may not share your tastes.

WHO TO INVITE—AND HOW?

When confronted with the task of assembling a list of invitees, the best man's first thoughts are: "Easy; invite the gang, right?" Not quite. If the groom is like most men, he has friends from his hometown, high school, college, and work. Rarely do they all know each other. So the best man has to consult the groom—assuming this isn't a total surprise (which is a bad idea)—and get those names and numbers.

You can divide the evening into two parts if you or the groom feel that half of the participants want to drink all night and ogle babes while the other half wants good steaks. If that's the case, start with dinner and drinks and dedicate the latter part of the evening to the debauchery so uninterested parties may leave early. The idea is to please the groom-to-be, not you and your buddies.

tip: If it's a long evening party, make sure you've scheduled a food break somewhere.

How Many People?

Fewer than six people and you have a get-together, not a party. This is fine, but it's not going to make for wild times. Most bachelor parties involve between eight and twenty participants. Any more, and you have to contend with a number of hassles: coordi-

Tales of Whoa #1:

X-Rated Snake Charming

One record executive had no idea what to expect. He was literally blindfolded and brought to a 2,500-square-foot space where twenty-five of his friends had congregated to consume plentiful booze and admire fifteen stunning strippers. The best man set up a makeshift VIP lounge with blue lights, couches, and a tarp to hide the action. All it took was one stripper to whip out a prop—in this case a dildo—and the place lit up. The real crowd-pleasers, of course, were the women who performed unusually cunning stunts. One stripper placed a condom on the groom's foot, and then guided his foot into her. Another stripper inserted a black rubber snake inside her—and waited for the most daring guy in the crowd to remove it using his teeth.

nating the arrival of so many people, finding a space to accommodate them all, traveling from one location to another, baby-sitting drunks, and trying to fit in face time for everyone with the groom—he is, after all, the reason everyone has come.

Who Makes the Cut?

The groom decides. He should not (nor should you) feel compelled to invite every male attending the wedding. This is *his* big night and you might have to remind him to keep the list down to fifteen or so people—not twenty-five or thirty-five. Smaller parties are easier to coordinate, can change plans quickly and easily, and

*"I'm not rejecting you, Dad. I just said that an evening
like this is very, very straight."*

have less bickering about what's next. Large parties, however, can afford to explore more expensive activities. Invite a few more than you really want since you will inevitably receive a lot of maybes and a few "can't-make-its." Have a few "second string" invitees just in case you need to add more bodies (or cash) to the party.

Remember that anyone invited to the bachelor party will assume they have also been invited to the wedding and/or reception—so don't invite some people just to the party unless there's a good reason (the groom is eloping, he's eloped, it's family only, or he's keeping the wedding itself small for whatever the reason). One other point to consider: If a guest does not speak English—like an in-law from a foreign country—he may not be able to appreciate the festivities, especially if it involves karaoke and comedy clubs. This can be one more way to cut the list: Delete people who just won't have fun, for whatever the reason (like a Darwinian survival of the funnest).

Remind the groom that those friends and family members who don't attend the bachelor party will have ample time to make fools of themselves at the reception after the wedding.

If you must have surprise visitors, they should be good old friends from out of town or the "entertainment" themselves (assuming they won't offend or embarrass the groom).

Family Members?

Perhaps the toughest question is: Do you invite family members? Invite the bride's brother and you risk having a close family member see you at your lowliest and most unattractive . . . or don't invite him and he'll think you're rude, forgetful, or both. The same goes for dads, uncles, and so on.

The Man Show's Adam Carolla summed it up in an article for Playboy.com:

*The problem is that you have witnesses. And, even if the
dad or the brother of the bride doesn't repeat it immediately, there's still the fact that they're walking around
with that information and they could use it at any point in
the relationship.*

It's up to the groom to decide if any family members attend.
Clearly, the brother of the groom will be present—he may even be
the best man. But the bride's brother? Only if he's close to the
groom, he's flown in from a foreign city/country, or the groom will
get a guilt trip for not inviting him. Your best bet is to include men
of the groom's age/generation and not those who are significantly
older or younger (unless you are planning a big family reunion or
cross-generational bonding session). And if it's going to be an
R-rated party, just leave borderline cases off the list. Better they
get offended by the lack of invitation than by the sight of the
groom drinking shots off the stripper's navel.

Women?

If you invite a woman to a bachelor party, it's not a textbook
bachelor party. You've lost the sense of shameless and uninhibited
male camaraderie. In some cases, there are gals who are "one of the
guys." If the groom wants her present, let her come. She probably
knows what he and his friends are capable of, anyway.

What Kind of Invitation—E-mail, Phone, or Printed Card?

Formal printed cards are unnecessary unless you're planning a
swanky bachelor party. You may still want to send something in
hard copy. Creative types might like to make their own theme invites, assuming this doesn't seem too Martha Stewart-esque. Ex-

trivia: In the second episode of *Laverne & Shirley*, Laverne rents out her father's pizza joint to Fonzie for a bachelor party and persuades Shirley to serve Fonzie's guests while Laverne makes pizzas. When the party backfires, the girls are called upon to help Fonzie save face—Shirley has to jump out of the cake.

amples: If it's a golf weekend, get some cheap golf paraphernalia together (golf ball, tee) and pack them into a small bag or pouch along with the invite. If it's a cigars-and-Scotch dinner, throw in a good cigar and swizzle stick. Get creative. Or just send a card/ email with the following details:

Joe Blow's Bachelor Party
Location
Address
Date/Time
Directions
Notes:
What you'll be doing (activity list)
What the local accommodations are like (if staying overnight)
How much this costs (per person)
What to wear (formal or not?)
What to bring (gifts, equipment, booze, food for barbecue?)
RSVP number with deadline for RSVPing

Phone calls are time consuming and hard to manage. There will be initial calls and then follow-ups and then last-minute reminders. The best bet is to use an e-mail system or Web-based invite. Some, like the ones offered at *evite.com,* allow the user to do the following:

1. Create an invitation that includes all the details about the party: when, where, etc.
2. Include a map with the invite.
3. Send out mass mailings in one batch process.
4. Track the RSVPs on-line
5. Initiate and manage discussions about the party among the invitees to discuss what to wear, what they're bringing, fees, etc.
6. Post updates as needed.
7. Keep the site as an on-line memento of the event, years after the party.

When to Invite?
Give everyone at least four weeks.

Follow-Through
No matter how you contact the invitees, you will need to keep track of RSVPs. This can be done with computer programs (Microsoft Word, Excel, Access), notepads, or Web-based invitation systems (*evite.com*). Do not wing it and hope you remember who said they would attend. The record keeping can also include notes about who has paid their dues, who's arriving late, who's bringing what, and other planning details.

tip: Remember to *exclude* the groom's e-mail address if you hope to surprise him with any of the party details and/or if you plan to discuss gifts on the site.

Tales of Whoa: #2

May the Best Man Lose

If you're thinking about inviting your dad to your bachelor party, this might change your mind. At a bachelor party in New York City, the groom's dad showed up in a mellow mood. The gent proceeded to down a few drinks, and his mood quickly went from mellow to mayhem. When the stripper arrived, Dad wanted a piece of the action and actually got into a scuffle with the best man over who would score with the stripper. The groom's dad clocked the best man and left the party with the stripper.

Reservations and Confirmation

You cannot reconfirm enough. This goes for the hotel room, the limo, the talent, and everything else that's left to others to provide. Confirm reservations one week before the party. Then call again the day before the big event. You don't want any surprises.

In one disastrous bachelor party, a group of men decided to kayak down a river in Alaska for one week. They chose a remote spot that was accessible only with a helicopter. On the first day of the trip, the men were dropped off at the predetermined spot and watched the helicopter fly away. After just a few hours, they realized that no one had confirmed the delivery of the kayaks, which were supposed to have been dropped off nearby. The equipment never arrived and they spent the week camping in the same place they were deposited.

"AND MY THIRD WISH IS THAT ALL THIS BE TAX EXEMPT."

How Much Will It Cost?

The simple answer: More than you ever think. Probably double.

The more complete answer: It depends on what you plan to do. The key thing to remember: Create a budget. Divide it by the number of guys you have *minus the groom* (he shouldn't pay for a thing all night). And tell everyone to bring at least $25 more than that.

A big mistake is thinking that it's going to be a simple $50 or $100 night for a steak dinner and a few drinks. Most men forget that they have to chip in for all the groom's drinks, entertainment, food, transportation, and gratuities—plus hotel and stripper (if applicable). The best man, or planner, absolutely must calculate the total in advance and *explain* this total to the guys when he invites them. Some bachelor parties may be prohibitively expensive for some men and it's better they decline in advance so that they aren't put in a position where they feel cheap, or worse, feel compelled to pay the equivalent of a month's rent—begrudgingly at best.

At one party I attended, about half of the guys knew and understood they would be paying for certain stimulating drugs. The other half—including me—didn't think we needed anything more than a few beers to have a good time (especially locked up in a hotel room with a bunch of other men). The best man nearly had a fit when some of the guys refused to pay for substances they didn't want. This could easily have been avoided.

Below is a list of common items found at bachelor parties, be-

tip: Remind everyone that even a prix-fixe meal will cost extra if everyone drinks booze.

fore, during, and after the festivities. Don't forget that all good parties have pricey aftermaths too (think: hunger and hangover).

Sample Inventory List

PG-Rated Parties
- Limousine: 4 hours @ $85/hr: $340 (plus tip: $68)
- Cigars: Robusto (Dominican) Cohibas, box of 25: $75
- Steak dinner: $100 per person
- Scotch and champagne: $50 per person and up
- Polaroid camera: $50 (you don't want anyone else processing these pics)
- Polaroid film, 10 rolls @ $13 each: $130
- (See "PG-Rated Activities" for a detailed account of pricing for various activities.)

R-Rated Parties
- Strip club: $20 cover and $20 to $40 per person for a lap dance and yet another $20 for drinks—minimum
- 2 strippers for 1 hour @ $300 per stripper: $600
- Tip, if they earned it @ $50 per stripper: $100
- Limousine: 4 hours @ $85/hr: $340 (tip $68)
- Cigars: Robusto (Dominican) Cohibas, box of 25: $75
- 2 bottles Jim Beam: $36
- 2 bottles Stoli vodka: $34
- 3 twelve-packs of Foster's: $30
- 2 bottles Cuervo tequila: $28
- Soft drinks: $8.00
- Dirty movie rentals (3): $9.00
- 3 large, delivered pizzas: $48
- Hotel room: $169

- Aerosol whipped cream: $4
- Chocoholics body frosting: $12.95

The Unforeseen
- Reassuring calls to girlfriends/wives: 10 @ $.35 = $3.50
- Rug cleaner, bottle: $3.00
- Professional carpet cleaning for 10 × 15-foot room: $45
- Acquiring original copy of videotape to destroy: variable
- Condoms: $10
- Mints: $2.00

The Morning After
- Two aspirin: 50 cents (restaurant package)
- Restaurant Bloody Mary: $4.00
- Two eggs, sausage, toast: $2.99

GRATUITY GUIDE: WHAT TO TIP

The bachelor party should be a night to remember—or forget—depending on what exactly transpires. Either way, this costs money. And it doesn't matter if you're the best man or you barely know the groom—everyone's got to chip in the same.

The best man no doubt calculated the fees for the hotel room and cigars and so on. But one thing always gets lost in the shuffle: the tips. At the very least, you've got to tip the waiter, the bar-

tip: Tell everybody to bring cash. This saves the best man from shelling out for the incidentals (cabs, tips, extra beer, whatever) and it helps the guys budget their night.

Tales of Whoa: #3

Saturday Night Peever

At one bachelor party, the best man organized a major theme for the party: He wanted to rock the groom's world by going to *the* Brooklyn disco where *Saturday Night Fever* took place. They rented a limo and took fifteen guys out to this outer borough. Just as they were paying to get in, they noticed that it was now a gay bar. Because they had traveled so far and had no other plan, they went in anyway and spent the whole night there. Not what they had expected.

tender, and the entertainer(s). If you're attending a mega-event of a party, you'll be dealing with coat checks and chambermaids and bellboys and cabbies—and maybe even a blackjack dealer. Do you know how much to tip each of them?

Hook them up and they will hook you up. But remember: If you can't afford to tip, you should just stay home and rent Tom Hanks's *Bachelor Party.*

Waitperson: Waiters and waitresses get 15 to 20 percent, depending on quality of service—you can veer low if the booze amounts to a major portion of the bill. Did they whet your appetite? Make your meal better in some unexpected but tangible way? Or just downright flirt? Throw them some extra cash for making you feel good. Make it 20 percent at a four-star restaurant or for parties of six or more. Never shoot the messenger. If your food isn't good or takes forever to arrive, the blame most likely falls on the kitchen, and complaints should be made to the manager, not taken out on the wait staff.

Bartender: One dollar per drink or 20 percent if running a tab. If the bartender comps you a round of drinks, tip half of what the drinks would have cost. You might get another free round.

Sommelier: Wine snobs will tell you to leave 10 to 15 percent of the wine bill, but if you tip the waitperson kindly, generally speaking, money will make its way to where it belongs (some sommeliers get a separate salary and some are included in a tip pool).

Host/Maître d': Nada, unless special services are provided, such as getting you a special table or amending a menu selection to meet your dietary requests. Then you can slap a ten spot in his hand with a heartfelt thank you.

Coat Check: A buck a coat.

Bathroom Attendant: Throw 'em 50 cents or a dollar. Make the most of your money and smell a bunch of those colognes while you're there. Add sparingly.

Concierge: Ten dollars—regardless of the length of your stay—and more if they finagle restaurant reservations or overlook your personal indiscretions. Nothing if you two never spoke.

Bellboy: At four-star hotels, it's $5.00 for opening and showing the room and another $5.00 or $10 for carrying one or two bags/suitcases to your room. Elsewhere, a buck a bag should do.

Chambermaid: Three dollars a day for Motel 6–type joints, $5.00 a day for swank hotels.

Room Service: These days, 15 percent of the bill usually appears on the check so remember to look before adding, or not adding, more.

Airline Skycaps: A buck a bag. Here's one person you don't want to upset. They have your luggage.

Cabbie: Fifteen percent of the fare is fine. Big spenders should round up.

Limo Driver: He gets 20 percent because he not only drove you to and from your destinations, but he suggested some local haunts, ignored the hooting and hollering coming from the back of the car, and patiently waited for you guys to return stinking drunk.

Valet: These guys have your car—so don't be cheap. Most people pay $1.00 a car; $3.00 may get you better service, but who knows?

Sports Arena Usher: One dollar per party if shown to your seat (this seems like a bargain considering you're shelling out four bucks per wiener).

Strippers: An average lap dance runs about 20 bucks and up, so the tip shouldn't be less than five bucks . . . more if she gets your lap really dancing.

Dancers at Bachelor Parties: Dancers receive a flat rate for performing but should be tipped 20 percent; any extra effort on her part should be generously rewarded.

Blackjack, Poker, and Roulette Dealer: Five-dollar chip per session, win or lose.

Cocktail Waitresses: Look at what these women are wearing for God's sake, and pay the standard dollar a drink.

---

celebrity trivia: Two midgets wore diapers at Jimmy Stewart's bachelor party at the legendary Beverly Hills restaurant called Chasen's in 1949.

What to Tip Quick Guide

Airline Skycaps: $1.00 per bag.

Bartender: $1.00 per drink or 20 percent if running a tab.

Bathroom Attendant: 50 cents or a dollar.

Bellboy: $1.00 per bag.

Blackjack, Poker, and Roulette Dealer: $5.00 chip per session, win or lose.

Cabbie: 15 percent of fare.

Chambermaid: $3.00 to $5.00 a day.

Coat Check: $1.00 per coat.

Cocktail Waitress: $1.00 per drink.

Concierge: $10 if he or she helped a lot.

Dancers at Bachelor Parties: 20 percent of flat rate.

Host/Maître d': Nada.

Limo Driver: 20 percent of total.

Room Service: 15 percent of bill (it's often included).

Sommelier: Rarely needed.

Sports Arena Usher: $1.00 per party if shown to your seat.

Valet: $3.00 minimum.

Waitperson: 15% to 20% of bill.

Limousines 101

If you don't want to assign a designated driver for a bachelor party, this is the only other way you guys can party without risking lives. No gala event should rely on public transportation— unless that's somehow designed to be part of the fun (i.e., some guys may indeed revel in the idea of parading the groom-to-be around in his underwear on a bus at 3 A.M.). However, buses and trains do not usually make for great party spaces.

So unless everyone's shipping out to a resort (or partying in Manhattan), it's best to plan for a limo service. These are the questions you should be asking yourself and, in some cases, the limo companies in your area:

- How much for a night and how many hours does that include?
- What is provided gratis in the limo (champagne, soda, liquor, TV, radio, tape, and/or CD player)?
- Are tip, taxes, and/or tolls included in the fee?
- How many people fit in the car?
- What's allowed (open sunroof, smoking, strippers in the car, etc.)?

HOW MUCH FOR A NIGHT AND WHAT HOURS DOES THAT INCLUDE?

First, you cannot rent a limo for one hour unless you're going to the airport. The minimum is usually three hours, sometimes more. Find out before you book it.

Pricing depends on several factors:

- Size and type of vehicle
- Day of week
- Time of year
- Geographic region
- Company policy

The bigger it is, the pricier it gets. Generally speaking, you'll find rates between $50 and $200 per hour. Some vehicles are decked out with in-car entertainment and some aren't. If you want to play your own mix during the driving portions of the party,

tip: Make sure that an "all-inclusive" fee covers the total fare plus taxes, tolls, local calls, booze, and everything but the tip. Some companies will feel you out and try to charge extra—at the end of the night—for bogus state taxes, beverages, and other miscellaneous minutiae.

make sure the limo has a tape or cd player. Maybe there's a VCR/ DVD player too. If you have a long ride at any time, think about what you can do inside the limo besides drinking.

Weekends cost more than weekdays. Proms, weddings, Spring Break, and holidays jack the prices up during March, April, May, and early June. Big cities like New York and San Francisco can charge more than smaller cities like Phoenix. And different companies can charge whatever they like, so shop around. But remember that lower prices might bring you more headaches like late limo arrival, no-shows, crappy vehicles, or no insurance. Go with a reputable company.

Tipping is extra—around 20 percent of the total bill. Sometimes, it's included in the stated fee—which is good for the driver and for you since you're quite likely to blow extra cash on more women and booze. And if anyone deserves a tip, it's the guy who drove you around for hours, told you where to go, and put up with your questionable behavior.

And yes, you do have to pay for the time the limo is *not* being used. It can't go anywhere else while you're partying inside some club or bar, so you're renting the driver's time, as well as the vehicle.

tip: Tell the limo company why you need the car. The owners and drivers know the city better than you do. They take bachelors out all year long. Not only do they have good ideas, they may cut you a deal or at least let you know about a "bachelor package" that includes extra booze or strippers.

HOW MANY PEOPLE FIT IN THE CAR?

The most common limos and stretch limos are listed below, but not every limousine company offers such a wide range. Most luxury sedans are Lincoln Town Cars or Cadillacs. But the stretch limo market has boomed in recent years. I've seen stretch Mercedes, Corvettes, Mustangs, Lexuses, Navigators, and Hummers.

Size Chart and Approximate Hourly Rates

- 6-passenger stretch limousines ($40–$60)
- 8-passenger stretch limousines ($50–$85)
- 10-passenger stretch limousines ($60–$100)
- 12–18-passenger limousines ($85–$150)
    These are usually stretch SUVs like Excursions and Hummers.
- VIP Party Coach: $100–$200
    Sure, it looks like a shuttle bus. Still, it may offer a veritable nightclub on wheels. You can probably stand up in it and so can the strippers.

At one Vegas limo company, VIP Transportation Services (also known as Xclusive Vegas Limos, *www.xclusivevegaslimos.com,*

800-835-4248), party planners can request the full bachelor party package. Here, the driver is also the DJ. He will drive the vehicle for eight hours, with a full open bar all night (hard liquors and beers and mixers—no champagne), complementary admission to Crazy Horse Too gentleman's club, and VIP Line passes to clubs in town (no waiting in line). This package costs $1,500 and accommodates about fifteen guys. Tip is extra. Daytime is cheaper than nighttime; weekdays are cheaper than weekends (Thursdays count as weekends). The nights, however, are better on weekends in Vegas. Custom packages can be put together, too.

WHAT'S ALLOWED—AND WHAT'S NOT? (OPEN SUNROOF, SMOKING, DRUGS?)

Limo drivers have the right to request no smoking. But they rarely care since they know many bachelors will smoke cigars. Drinking is par for the course, and most limos come stocked with liquor. Anything harder (and/or illegal) is a risk. But generally speaking, the drivers advocate a "don't ask, don't tell" policy: The partiers can do what they like, but the driver may not join in the fun.

Paid escorts and strippers are usually allowed to perform in the limo. If she's expected to perform "extra" duties on the groom, the other guys must leave the limo. The driver, almost always, should

tip: To save money, but still provide transportation, consider renting a van, which can easily carry ten people. You'll need a designated driver, of course, but it's far cheaper than renting a limo for the night.

remain in the front seat of the car so there are no issues of non-consent and no rough stuff.

National Limo Web Sites

www.limo-search.com
www.limousines.com
www.1800limo.com
www.1800bookalimo.com

Cigars 101

Even if they are not as trendy as they once were, they're a welcome addition to any bachelor party. You need to know what brands are especially reliable/good, how to cut and light cigars, how much they cost and when to break them out.

How Do You Choose?

Inevitably, one of your know-it-all buddies will tell you to go with Cubans. They are, of course, illegal and—even worse—highly overrated. What's more, few if any of your friends would recognize a true Havana cigar even if Castro himself showed up at the party and rolled his own. Keep in mind that many non-Cuban cigars have swiped the names of Cuban classics, such as Cohiba, Punch, and Partagas (and there is always the possibility that you will end up purchasing moldy, old, and/or counterfeit ones).

Don't be fooled into thinking you stumbled across an affordable box of Cubans at your local smoke shop. Save yourself money, time, and trouble, and go with a more sensible purchase.

Which Countries Make Good Cigars?

There are four major cigar-producing nations besides Cuba: Nicaragua, the Dominican Republic, Costa Rica, and Honduras. Sure, Mexico, Jamaica, and Brazil offer up some fine smokes too, but you're better off sticking with the heavies. Each country's cigars have their own characteristics. Nicaraguans are strong stogies, Dominicans tend to be more mild, while Costa Ricans and Hondurans are somewhere in the middle.

Mild or Strong?

When I refer to mild and strong cigars, I'm talking about the flavor and aroma of the smoke; a strong cigar won't be any harsher in your mouth. A mild-tasting smoke can still stay with you like that last can of cheap beer, while a powerful, heavy cigar's taste can disappear quicker than you'd expect.

What Size?

There are several sizes of premium cigars. For this special occasion, you want something substantial, but not huge: a Robusto or Corona should do the trick. Churchills look cool—they are huge—but are endless challenges to the lungs.

Do Wrappers Matter?

Yes. The cigar wrapper refers not to the plastic packaging around it, but to the leaf in which the tobacco is rolled. Wrappers generally fall into two categories: Claro, which is light-colored and mild, and Maduro, which is dark and heavy. Novices should start out with Claro.

A FEW FINAL BITS OF ADVICE

- Bring plenty of matches or a lighter.
- Bring a cigar cutter or two.
- If no one's an expert, ask the tobacconist for suggestions.
- It doesn't really matter what you buy, because most people are happy just to have a cigar.

How to Cut and Light a Cigar

If you're paying $20 for a cigar, you ought to treat it right. This can be the difference between a smooth, satisfying smoke and a serious drag. Do it wrong and the cigar will go out prematurely, burn down one side, go out too often, or require Herculean breaths. Different people favor different cigar cutters. One thing everyone agrees on: don't chomp off the end with your teeth.

There are five types of cigar cutters:

• The Guillotine

Yes, it's a miniature flat blade that literally chops off the head of the cigar. Chop at the point where the curved end starts to straighten out and make it one swift, clean motion to avoid crushing the end. The paper band can stay on or off, but most people I know keep it on because it keeps the cigar from crumbling and it reminds you of what brand you're smoking.

- **Scissors**

  You can find some very fancy scissors-shaped cigar cutters for hundreds of dollars, but these are no more effective than the guillotine—especially if you're smoking for just one night.

- **The Punch or Bullet**

  It may look like an actual bullet, but it functions more like a plunger, digging into the cigar and plucking out a plug of tobacco.

- **The "V" or Wedge**

  If you use a wedge-shaped blade, you'll want to cut a "V" into the head, but make sure it's not too deep. Cigar chewers should avoid this because they could conceivably make the cigar collapse and thus close up the draw. This doesn't work on certain oddly shaped cigars like the conical pyramids.

- **The Pierce**

  Some folks like to bore a sharp hole into the center of the head. Leave this to experts or you may wind up with an uneven draw or condensed bitter tobacco juice.

LIGHTING A CIGAR

A few simple pointers will save you from burning the cigar. First, use a lighter if you can since you'll likely need enough time to get the thing going. Make it a butane lighter since anything else will contaminate the flavor (even candle wax). If you must use matches, try wood matches, which last longer. Avoid sulfur at all costs. The best bet is to use a cigar lighter, which offers a fatter flame (or two flames simultaneously) and should have adjustable flame height.

Next, bring the cigar up to the flame, but not touching it, and light the end while slowly rolling the cigar between your thumb and forefinger so that all points of the end are exposed to the flame. Now stick it in your mouth (the cigar) and continue twirling it in your hand as you puff so it lights evenly. Go ahead and take a look at the end to make sure the whole thing is lit and not just one side. Continue to draw and light until your cigar is burning consistently all the way around. Remember: Don't inhale.

tip: If you want to avoid cigar stench, let the cigar burn out in an ashtray—don't snub it out. Once burnt out, toss it immediately in the trash.

RECOMMENDED CIGARS

Don't know which cigars or cigar shapes to buy for the big day? Each company makes cigars with various names and sizes. Churchills are large and therefore usually cost more than the smaller Corona size. Don't get anything smaller than a Corona unless you're in a rush. Taste is important too: If you're having Scotch and dinner, go with a stronger flavor. Price, too, will be a factor. If these guys smoke more cheeba than Cohibas, opt for a less expensive box. Following is a range of cigars and corresponding prices (the prices vary based on availability, the number of cigars pur-

Cigar Name	Shape	Average Price (Per Cigar)
Arturo Fuente	Robusto	$9.00
Ashton	Double Corona	$10
Cohiba	Churchill	$30
Davidoff	Churchill	$18
Dunhill	Robusto	$6.00
H. Upmann	Churchill	$5.00
Macanudo	Prince Phillip	$7.00
Montecristo #2	Pyramid	$23
Opus X	Toro	$13
Padron	Robusto	$13
Partagas	Double Corona	$23
Punch	Torpedo	$9.00
Romeo y Julieta	Churchill	$5.00

chased, and the whims of local merchants). The estimates listed are *per cigar*. You can probably get a better deal if you purchase a whole box. Buy only from reputable sources. Restaurants and strip clubs charge a lot more than cigar shops.

Booze 101

Even if you decide to throw the tamest, most subdued bachelor party ever, you'll probably drink alcohol—lots of it. When presented in the proper context, drinking can be elegant, sophisticated, and even educational. At least that's what you'll tell the bride. Why not make the party an opportunity for a tasting?

BOOZY ACTIVITIES FOR ELEGANT AFFAIRS

Every guy has a favorite drink. And yet few have tried them all. Bachelor parties are a great opportunity to see who knows what by hosting an alcohol-related activity (see more specific explanations in the "PG-Rated Activities" section). Here are some examples:

Hire a Bartender to Make Fancy Cocktails

You can hire a pro for the evening and not worry about making a mess—or learning cocktail recipes. Does everyone know what a Martini, Gibson, Sidecar, Gimlet, and Collins tastes like? Or how to make them? Now you can learn. Most pros will bring and return their own glasses too. Thus, no washing.

Host a Wine or Beer Tasting

Buy five kinds of Merlots and compare them. Or perform this ritual with Cabernet Sauvignons, Pinot Noirs, Chardonnays, stouts, lagers, ales, etc. Someone needs to lead, which means you either hire an expert or do some homework. Blind taste tests are fun since all the guys will want to prove how discerning their taste buds are. By the end of night, you will not only learn a lot—you will be very drunk.

Host a Scotch Tasting

See "Scotch Tasting" on page 106 for a complete step-by-step description of how to do this.

Learn How to Match Food and Wine

This will take some planning since most guys don't have the patience to match wine and food; some never knew (or cared) you could. Consult your local gourmet restaurant and see if they can work out a deal for your party. French restaurants are your best bets or check out a book or Web site that lists good matches and buy all the cheeses, meats, and snacks that go well with the wine you'd like to try.

FUNDAMENTAL SPIRITS

- Beer
- Wine (Sangria, Wine Coolers)
- Gin (Gimlet, Tonic, Martini, Ginger Ale, etc.)
- Vodka (Screwdriver, Cape Codder, Martini, Black Russian, etc.)
- Rum (Punch, Daiquiri, Pina Colada, Scorpion)
- Whiskey/Bourbon/Scotch (Manhattan, Old-Fashioned, Mint Julep, Irish Coffee, Rob Roy)
- Tequila (Tequila Sunrise)

DON'T FORGET:

- Mixers: 7-Up, club soda, tonic water, orange juice, grapefruit juice, Coke, cranberry juice, tomato juice
- Garnish: lemons, limes, olives, onions, maraschino cherries
- Details: Ice cubes, napkins, toothpicks, bottle openers

Nine Bachelor Party Drinking Games

If you're like most adults, you look back on drinking games as wonderful college-era fun—but, hopefully, something you out-grow by twenty-one (when you're finally legal). "Quarters" gets a little tiresome; and who knows where that quarter has been? But for bachelor parties, drinking games can make the night. They are

> *tip:* Don't put champagne in the freezer—ever. You'll wait forever to defrost it and it could ruin the bubbly altogether.

especially useful as a distraction in between events; while you're waiting for delivery of the pizza . . . or the stripper. And if you're really strapped for cash—and imagination—you could even make drinking games the evening's festivities.

Below are nine games that are especially well suited for bachelor parties. They don't require props, they don't assume coed groups, they don't force players to memorize arcane jargon, they don't involve keeping score, and they're neither pathetically familiar nor plain dumb. They are easy to learn and easy to start and stop. All require beer. Lots of beer.

1. Movie Cues

The possibilities are endless with this game. All you need is a movie, VCR/DVD player, and booze. In the event that you're watching the movie *Swingers,* for example, you might announce before the film's begun that everyone must drink whenever a character says "You're so money." If you want to drink more often, just agree on other drink cues. Here are some options. Use any or all.

DRINK . . .

a. whenever a certain person enters the scene

b. whenever there's nudity

c. whenever a character repeats a common phrase ("D'oh!")

2. Russian Beer Roulette or Beer Hunter

Two guys prepare a case of beer by removing one can. The first guy turns away as the second guy shakes the can as hard as he can so it's ready to spew. He places it back in the case. The first guy turns back and rearranges the cans just to make sure that not even the second guy knows where the booby-trapped can lies. Then, as each guy in the party grabs a can, he opens it in the direction of his own face. One man will get sprayed. The others can just drink. Repeat with the next case of beer.

3. Minute by Minute or Sixty Seconds or the Hour of Power

Every guy gets a shot glass. Every minute every guy must chug a shot of beer. Set a timer of some sort to remind everyone. Go ahead and chitchat or watch a movie in the process. The drinking starts slowly and innocently. No problem, right? Now play for sixty minutes. You will soon be very, very drunk.

4. Guessing Game

Fill a pitcher of beer. Take a sip as big or as small as you like. Then pass it along. The goal is to be the person who finishes the pitcher—and not the guy just before the guy who finishes it. If you finish it, you are the winner. You don't have to pay for another beer. If you are the guy who passes the pitcher to the winner, you lose. You have to buy the next pitcher. This can be played with all kinds of penalties for the loser and prizes for the winner.

5. Black or Red?

This requires one deck of cards and unlimited beer. Shuffle the deck. Remove the jokers. Place the deck face down on a table. The first person guesses whether the card on the top of the deck is black or red. If he's right, he doles out drinks to as many or as few people as he likes, based on the number of the card. So if it was a black six (club or spade), he "allows" six drinks to be sipped by others—in multiples of his choice. If he was wrong—it was a red three (heart or diamond), for example—he must drink three sips himself.

6. Letters

Someone starts by thinking of a letter in the alphabet. The next player must name a word that starts with that letter. Easy enough. Now it goes around the table, again and again as players name words that begin with that letter. The loser is the first person who cannot name a new word—often he cannot name a word at all. He drinks and the play resumes with a new letter. At a bachelor party, you can narrow down the pool of possible words by specifying that they must be, for example, parts of the female anatomy or curse words (including vernacular and slang). The game can also be played using rhymes, instead of same-letter series.

7. Smile!

This one requires a large tablecloth and a woman—probably a willing stripper or other hired help. The tablecloth should be long enough on all sides to cover the laps of the participants. All the guys sit down after pulling down their trousers (underwear optional). The stripper then climbs under the table and does whatever she likes to the guys, one by one, until one of them smiles. He has to drink. Play can continue endlessly or can be rigged so the groom quickly sports a proud, beaming smile.

8. 21

This is a customizable game, which can be adapted to make fun of or celebrate the groom—or any other players. One person starts by calling out the number 1. The player to his left goes next by saying 2. And so it goes. If someone screws up the order, they have to drink. When a player reaches 21, he gets to invent a rule. This is where the fun starts. He can require everyone to drink only with the left hand. Or replace 3 with 7. Or rule out multiples of 3. Or scream the name of the groom's ex-girlfriend before drinking. Or say, "[groom's name] is a knucklehead" before drinking. Etc. If someone screws up a rule, he drinks. Play begins again at 1 and continues to 21, at which time a new rule may be made.

9. Titanic

Divide the room into four teams. Fill one pitcher with beer—but only three-quarters full. And fill one cup or glass halfway up with beer. Place this glass inside the pitcher so it floats. Now, the teams take turns pouring as much or as little beer as they want into the cup. The team that sinks the cup drinks the pitcher. Repeat as needed.

WHEN THINGS GO TOO FAR

Who's Responsible If You Trash the Place While Drunk?

Whether it's a hotel or a bar, someone's gonna have to clean up if there's an overindulger (puker), a brawl, or some spills. Chances are hotel management won't notice if it's just a messy bathroom, clogged toilet, stained carpet, chipped furniture, or cigarette burn. However, you will be held liable—and they have your credit card on file—if you break the TV, toss anything out of the window, set fire to any part of the room, steal anything more valuable than soap, or break a wall or window. No matter what shape you leave the room in, try to leave at least a $5 tip for the chambermaid. She's gonna have a helluva time cleaning up after you.

Tales of Whoa: #4

Why Wait?

At most bachelor parties, things don't start getting crazy until the stripper shows up. But at this party, the best man couldn't wait. He started downing shot after shot and was so drunk he stripped down to his birthday suit in front of the other guys. By the time the stripper showed up, he was so pumped up he threw her over his shoulder and headed straight for the bedroom, leaving the rest of the party with no entertainment.

Don't Drink and Drive

This doesn't require an explanation. Just get a designated driver or limo. Or call for a cab.

How Not to Get Sick

Most of these preventative measures are common sense or at least part of urban folklore, but here goes:

a. Drink a glass of water in between every glass of alcohol.
b. Eat before you drink. I know I sound like a mom, but this is his last night of singlehood—not his last night of drinking. And no one likes a puker.
c. Drink light-colored liquors: Gin and vodka are safest.
d. Avoid dark drinks: Whiskey and red wine can do serious damage.

e. Steer clear of super-sweet drinks that require schnapps, cream-flavored liqueur, or lots of sugar.

f. Don't mix alcohols. Stick to the same drink all night.

g. Don't go to bed drunk—stay up a few hours more if possible.

h. Drink another glass of water.

i. Take two aspirins before you fall asleep. This is now controversial, but some people still believe in it. Advil seem to be better than Tylenol and other aspirins in this capacity. Some doctors believe that alcohol and aspirin are not a good mix. So consider asking a professional (a doctor, not a drunk) before trying this.

Hangover Remedies

There are loads of tricks. Some make sense because they require the suffering individual to eat food, which absorbs alcohol and replenishes nutrients. Others just rely on a hung-over person's gullibility in time of need or maybe just voodoo.

a. Hair of the dog: drink more alcohol—especially Bloody Marys.

b. Bad food: greasy burgers, fries, pizza, anything doughy.

c. Good food: bananas, tomatoes, or at least V-8.

d. Vitamins: take Vitamin B_{12} and/or Vitamin C.

e. Gatorade: tastes good too.

f. Caffeine: coffee or Coca-Cola. Coke is carbonated, and that helps the stomach too.

g. Water. You should always drink water and now's the time when your body cries out for hydration more than ever (alcohol dehydrates).

Last-Minute Bachelor Parties

So you waited until the very last second? Now you can't get a reservation at a fancy hotel, spa, golf course, restaurant, or casino. What's worse, your long-distance buddies can't get cheap flights.

We're not going to suggest you pull a Martha Stewart and create a pretty scrapbook to fake your thoughtfulness. But you do need a Plan B. And some of these ideas are good enough to be a Plan A.

Get Help

It's late. And you have to call twenty guys and tell them where to be, when, how to dress, and how much to bring. You can cut that time in half by splitting the duties with someone else. If you're smart, split the chores with many other people. Make a quick list of the guys you want to invite. Assign different tasks to the guys: gathering money, buying cigars, bringing booze, selecting a limo service, etc. Draw up a phone tree if there are more than twenty people; you call five guys and have them each invite four guys. In a word: delegate.

BYOB

It doesn't matter if you're planning a harmless camping trip or a night at Bada-Bing, guys will want to drink. Buy a six-pack for

bachelor saying: The reason men don't give the groom a shower, is that they figure he's all washed up anyway.

every guy. Or better, stock up on the basics: whiskey, gin, vodka, tequila, rum, Scotch, and mixers. Don't forget cups, bottle openers, and ice.

CONSIDER PG-RATED ACTIVITIES

You can partake in many of the suggested PG-rated activities quickly and easily. This includes last-minute steak dinners, barbecues, Scotch tastings, poker matches, pub-crawls, as well as trips to ballgames, casinos, and bowling alleys.

CONSIDER HOOTERS (IF YOU MUST)

Last we counted, there were more than three hundred Hooters restaurants (*www.hooters.com*) in forty-one states of the union—plus Asia, Canada, the Caribbean, South America, Europe, and Puerto Rico. They were practically made for bachelor parties and for obvious reasons . . . namely, the servers are girls with hooters. Call your local chapter to find out if they offer special group packages. Otherwise, it's worth considering for a drink or a bite—even as a lark (the company is fully aware of its questionable appeal; the official Web site refers to Hooters as "delightfully tacky, yet unrefined"). If you're lucky, the cheerleader-style girls will sing, jiggle, and sign T-shirts for you.

TRY NEW CLUBS AND DRINKS

This is your chance to experiment. First, you can go to all those bars and clubs you've been meaning to try. Money is no object tonight since all the guys will buy rounds for once. Ask the bartenders for their favorite obscure drinks and order them all. Buy some of the top-shelf Scotches, wines, and champagnes. Dig up

trivia: In 1982, two different companies released Breakout-like games titled Bachelor Party for the Atari 2600: Mystique/Swedish Erotica and PlayAround (which bundled Gigolo in the same package).

those old drinking games. And get to the bars early so you can find tables for your whole party. Depending on how naughty you want to get, the following actions may or may not be necessary:

- **Remind Everyone to Bring Cash**
  No matter what you do, you'll need it. Agree on a standard amount for everyone.

- **Make Reservations at a Steak House**
  Hey, they serve chicken and fish too, so no one has to opt out.

- **Buy a Box of Twenty-five Cigars**
  Go with a brand you've heard of or ask the local tobacconist.

- **Pick a Designated Driver**
  This may have to be you. Or else call for a limo.

- **Agree on a Crash Pad**
  Men's apartments only. This may be yours.

- **Go to a Night Club, Disco, or Strip Club**
  Bring cash—one- and twenty-dollar bills.

- **Go to a Hotel Room and Rent Naughty Videos**

   Don't bring home-videos—you never know what you've taped on to the end of one of those.

- **Consider Quick, Inexpensive Activities**

   It doesn't take more than a day to organize a barbecue, bowling night, poker match, wine tasting, pub crawl, or roast. Each constitutes a fine evening out, with no reservations needed.

TWO
PG-Rated Activities

Introduction

A bachelor party is more than just another boys' night out. It is a symbolic milestone, a celebration of the so-called last night of freedom, and a male-bonding ritual. But here's a little known secret: You don't have to get drunk, naked, or stupid. Sure, you could indulge in pleasures of the flesh; this book can help you do this quite well (see "R-Rated Activities" in Chapter 3). But it is not mandatory to visit a club, hire a stripper, or tie the groom naked to a lamppost. These days, it's all about having options. Do what's best for the groom.

Lucky for him, there are enough possibilities—even tame ones—to offer something for everyone. Outdoorsy and indoorsy types. Or parties suited to both. Rugged types might consider hunting, paintball, and stock-car racing. Urban types may lean toward poker, wine tasting, or steak and cigars. Combine the activities in a day-and-night celebration and you have a plan.

No matter what PG-rated plan you design, you'll avoid the horny-men-in-a-hotel-suite syndrome. Instead, you'll foster interaction among the guys—often from different cliques and with little in common besides knowing the groom. What's more, these activities allow for real conversation at a time when the impending marriage will unequivocally change the nature of the groom's friendships. Contemplation is inevitable. No wonder we see more and more bachelor parties partaking in travel, cross-country drives, sailing expeditions, mountain climbing, and bike marathons.

One more benefit: You can capture the moments on film/video for posterity. No hiding the evening's true unfolding of events, no lies to the fiancée, and no risk of getting a homely stripper. In other words: No regrets. That leaves more cash for food and drink anyway.

To make it easier to choose an activity for your party, I have organized the suggestions into three categories: Outdoorsy/Athletic, Swanky, Inexpensive.

Each receives a general explanation and then a quick look at some sample scenarios, costs, timing, photo opportunities, booze policies, and other minutiae. Sometimes, you can combine more than one of these activities. White-water rafting and mountain biking go well together, obviously. But you don't have to stop there. Why not add late-night poker and wine tasting to the itinerary—several hours after the daytime sports? And you can always do the naked chick thing later that night if you like.

PACKAGED ADVENTURE

If you search on-line for "bachelor party," you will inevitably stumble across companies that specialize in putting together activity packages for parties—corporate events, birthdays, bar mitzvahs, weddings, and so on. Some of these companies have expanded out of smaller businesses; fishing expeditions are often led by a captain who simply bought some more boats and started advertising. Talk to him to find out how long he's been doing what he does to gauge if he knows what he's doing.

On-line research can pinpoint the right company for your

party, based on quoted prices and phone personalities. Do not hire the first company you reach. Shop around, call for details, request brochures and/or videos. Ask if they've hosted bachelor parties and what to expect. Find out if they offer group discounts. Don't necessarily go with the least expensive company either; they may skimp on essentials. Try to get referrals or find trusted brands.

At the very least, you should look at company Web sites and ask the proprietors questions about what they offer. If nothing else, you'll get a sense of what other bachelor parties have done on boats, bikes, rivers, mountains, and golf courses in the past.

Some of these companies offer booze as part of their packages; others may not allow you to bring your own. Ask if the establishment allows and/or provides such amenities (you might ask about food and photographers as well). As an incentive for group parties, many companies won't charge the bachelor or will bill you for twenty people when there were twenty-one present. If they don't mention it, ask.

Three Major PG-Rated Categories

1. Outdoorsy/Athletic Activities
Fishing, Golfing, Camping/Climbing/Hiking/Rafting/Biking/Bonfire, Laser Tag/Paintball, Skydiving/Bungee Jumping, Major League Baseball Game, Dude Ranch/Hunting/Riflery, Skiing/Snowboarding, Car Racing/Bumper Cars/Tanks, Tournaments: Tennis/Basketball/Baseball/Football/Soccer/Volleyball

2. Swanky Activities
Gambling at Casinos, Massage/Spa Treatments, Resort Weekend, Steak (and Cigars), Cruise, Gambling at the Horse Track, Hiring Celebrity Look-Alikes

> *tip:* Read the contract if there is one. Ask for one or create one if there is none. The five minutes of faxing could save you hours of agony if there's a screw-up. This goes for caterers, bars, clubs, limos, entertainers, hotels, extreme sports facilities, and even fishing boats. You don't want any surprises. Take the time to go over the fine print and make sure that you're aware of cancellation policies and additional/hidden fees.

3. Inexpensive Activities

Barbecue, Bowling, Poker Basics, Scotch Tasting, Arcade/ Amusement Park, Pub Crawl, Host a Roast, Dancing/Clubbing, Karaoke, Scavenger Hunt

Outdoorsy/Athletic Activities

Nature offers plenty of logical alternatives to cramming twenty guys into a hotel suite full of smoke and beer. It doesn't matter if half the bachelor party has never golfed or camped before; the idea is to actively enjoy a picturesque setting. Sports parties combine some of the best aspects of male bonding; they immerse the guys in planned adventures that often require team effort. When guys go skydiving, for example, no one can sit in a corner and act bored. For many men, this will be a once-in-a-lifetime experience. Let's hope we can say the same thing about the wedding.

The price range varies from low-end camping and hiking trips to pricey weekend fishing/golfing/skiing/resort excursions. Don't forget to include incidentals in your estimate, such as equipment, transportation, food, instructor fees, and tips. And always bring plenty of water.

FISHING

If the mere mention of fishing expeditions conjures up images of Grandpa patiently waiting for the fish to bite, you're living in the wrong century. Modern men want more than a suntan and a few fish to eat at the end of the day. They want adventure and entertainment. And believe it or not, fishing can be a multifaceted experience, including sight-seeing, barhopping, swimming, snorkeling, and even watching the game (many ships have televisions nowadays). You can book a half-day or a full day, on a big or small vessel, staying near land or venturing out to sea. If nothing else, the groom gets to look like a hero with a photo of the largest catch of the day.

Sample Scenarios

In Seattle, you can fish for salmon, rock cod, flounder, and sea bass. Several companies in the area offer chartered fishing boats. All Seasons Charter Service (425-743-9590) is located in Edmonds, about fifteen miles north of Seattle, and charters out a forty-foot boat for $750 a day. Allstar Fishing Charters (425-252-4188/ *www.allstarfishing.com*) sends boats out from Everett (north of Edmonds) as well as from downtown Seattle. A seven-hour trip runs about $125 per person. License, bait, and tackle are included in the price, but you should BYOB (and food) because even the best bachelor party needs fuel.

Another Washington-based company (on Puget Sound), All Star Fishing Charters, specializes in catching salmon. They charge $130 per person for a standard seven-hour fishing trip; four-hour afternoon trips cost $400 for one to four people and $500 for five to six people. Everyone must pay for a $6.00 fishing license.

At Lake Michigan, there are more than a hundred different charter boats available for everything from a blues cruise with a live band to deep-lake fishing. During the summer months, you can fish for two kinds of salmon (king and silver), two kinds of trout (lake and steelhead), and various other critters. Most charter boats will provide everything you need (tackle, lines, rods) except the beer, and will take you out on the lake anywhere from two to eight hours. A six-hour charter will run you at least $400—not too bad if you split the costs among several guys.

More adventurous outdoor types might want to venture three and a half hours outside of Washington, D.C., to Escatawba Farms (540-962-6487) for some Montana-like fly-fishing in Virginia's Allegheny Mountains. You're guaranteed to catch (and then release) enormous rainbow trout. The company provides the gear and instruction for even the most novice anglers. Parties are limited to eight people, so it's never crowded (larger parties must look elsewhere). It's best to go in the fall when the leaves are changing color, but the fishing is open all year except during July and August. The cost is $50 per rod per day and $175 per day for a guide/instructor with lunch. They'll hook you up with a place to stay too; lodging price depends on whether you want a rustic cabin or a restored nineteenth-century house.

In Miami, the catch of the day is often barracuda and marlin some as large as 450 pounds. Dozens of fishing charters head for the seas every day. A full day out usually runs from 8 A.M. to around 4 P.M., with a full private charter costing around $750. But the party has to be small. The Coast Guard limits trips to six people per forty-five-foot boat. Some charters, like the Magic Fingers, specialize in live bait fishing. The peak summer months, July through September, are the best time for catching bottom dwellers like snapper and grouper. Bring along some live crab and lobster for the expedition—the snapper like it as much as we do.

One South Beach, Miami-based man who specializes in bachelor fishing parties—from ten to thirty-five passengers—is Captain Wayne (305-372-9470). He commands two vessels: one fifty-six feet and one seventy feet long. He is also licensed for ocean routes so you can go out farther and have larger parties. He can provide food and beverages, too, or you may bring your own. The boats have stereos, CD players, and a TV—great for watching sports. On his excursions, the party fishes for bigger fish using live bait; the groom usually takes home a fish as a trophy. Or Captain Wayne can arrange for local taxidermists to create a fiberglass replica based on the look and size of the fish caught. Video of the trip is also available—for no extra charge—but it's not professionally edited (the captain is the cameraman). Strippers are allowed, but be prepared to pay for four hours of their time. If it's pouring or the seas are too rough, you can go sight-seeing or take the guys to bars on the coast—Key Biscayne, Fort Lauderdale (for all-day trips). The only no-no's: drugs and swimming off the boat. It costs $1,200 for a half-day on the big seventy-foot boat (up to thirty-five people). The fifty-six-foot boat costs $600 for smaller parties. A 15 percent gratuity is expected.

Approximate Cost per Person? Depends on the size of the boat, time spent cruising/sailing, whether or not you are renting rods and buying bait, and how much food and booze you are consuming. Some boat owners will offer catering, beer, and even arrange for entertainment. You'll also need to spring for some supplies such as rain gear, sunblock, motion sickness medication, beach towels, jackets, and a cooler for your catch. Figure on spending $100 per person or more.

How Far in Advance Should You Plan? Ideally, more than four weeks in advance. If you're flexible, the captain can probably find a day and time that suits your needs.

Number of Days for Event? Half day or full day.

Photo or Video Ops? Classic groom shot: Him and his catch. Try to get the boat and water in the background. Some captains have their own still and video cameras. If not, you can always bring your own. Some people recommend disposable cameras so you won't pull your hair out when the camera gets lost or wet.

Booze Policy? Almost all allow beer; just don't plan on swimming.

GOLFING

Golfing is a gentleman's game. But you pay for the privilege. Public courses tend to be cheaper, though they are more crowded. Private clubs offer catering, private rooms, and a less harried golfing experience. Consider planning for an overnight stay in a small hotel to add to the festivities and obviate the need for the fellas to bring beer onto the course. Here are some suggestions around the country.

Sample Scenarios

Las Vegas has around fifty courses, most of which are open to the public—the wealthy public—but only on certain days of the week. Among the most esteemed is the high-end Shadow Creek Golf Club (866-260-0069), which features eighteen holes of bent grass, trees, and enough sand and water traps to ruin your life for a few hours. At Mirage Resorts (800-360-7111)—from Monday through Thursday only—the golf package goes for as high as $1,000 per person, which includes a night's stay at the Mirage, transportation to the course, a round of golf, a cart, and a caddy. Collared shirts are required; no denim (which should disappoint no one on a 115-degree afternoon). If shorts are worn, they must be Bermuda shorts. Call for other stipulations.

If you're near Chicago, head out to Lamont, Illinois. At Cog Hill Number Four (630-257-5872), site of the Great Western Open and Tiger Woods's first PGA win, you'll find a par 72, eighteen-hole course designed to be difficult but fair. It costs $100 per person and is one of the country's most scenic places to play.

Approximate Cost per Person? About $75 to $1,000 a day (not including cocktails and lunch).

How Far in Advance Should You Plan? Two weeks or more.

Number of Days for Event? One day on a public course; a weekend at a private resort.

Photo or Video Ops? Bring cameras, video cameras, and look to catch the groom teeing off, the guys decked out in golf gear, and at least a few shots of the course's scenery.

Booze Policy? Drink before or after.

CAMPING/CLIMBING/HIKING/RAFTING/BIKING/BONFIRE

If you go to a bachelor party where you will be camping, you don't just want to sit around a campfire and get drunk for the whole weekend. As a result, many of these excursions involve other outdoorsy activities. The beer can wait until the end of the day. If you do want to sit around and get drunk—somewhere in a natural setting rather than in a bar—consider a bonfire on the beach. Either way, you can blindfold the groom, take him away, and play whatever games you like. Maybe even bring music and make it an outdoor feast too.

Sample Scenarios

Many companies around the country act as one-stop shops for active sportsmen. Pocono Whitewater Rafting, located in Jim

Thorpe, PA, (800-WHITEWATER/*www.whitewaterrafting.com*) offers combinations of white-water rafting, kayaking, paintball, and mountain biking. You tell the coordinators about your party and they'll help arrange the perfect excursion.

Coordinators will need to know the following:

- How many people are on the trip?
- How many activities do you want to include in the time you are there?
- Which one or two activities are most important?
- What's the general skill level of the party attendees?
- What equipment are you bringing and what needs to be rented?

Approximate Cost per Person? Plan for $50 to $150 per person, if you use a guide or professional outdoor sports company. As always, it depends on whether you want a whole weekend or just a day trip. Remember to include gas, food, booze, tents, and equipment in your calculations.

At Pocono Whitewater Rafting, rafting costs $50 per person for a seven-hour day (twenty or more gets a discount) and the bachelor rafts for free. Biking is $25 and up for bike and shuttle service to and from the destination. Ask if the trip includes helmets, maps, water, parking, knapsacks, and/or binoculars. If not, you can always bring your own or rent these separately.

On the West Coast (in Northern California), a popular Sacramento-based company is W.E.T. (888-RAFTWET/*www.raft wet.com*). The folks here charge $115 per person for a day trip (shuttle, lunch, guide service) and $310 for a two-day package. You can arrange for rafting from class 3 (moderate) to 5 (expert). From May to August, you may have to book six months in ad-

tip: Bring lots of water. More than you think you'll need.

vance. For an extra fee, you can hire a photographer/videographer and upload the shots to your own Web site. No booze on the river.

How Far in Advance Should You Plan? At least four weeks. Up to six months in advance for rafting on weekends during the summer. Remember to have a backup plan in case it rains; these are usually overnight adventures and the weather can turn on you.

Number of Days for Event? One day, overnight, or a full weekend.

Photo or Video Ops? Most companies recommend you don't bring a camera onto the kayak or raft because you'll likely lose or damage it.

Booze Policy? No booze allowed when rafting or kayaking. A better bet is to find a lodge in the area and plan on dinner and drinks later that evening when you can get loose and not worry about falling out of a boat.

LASER TAG/PAINTBALL

If you thought football was the ultimate physical-primal-male-bonding activity, you haven't tried paintball. This is as close to hunting as most men will ever get—and you're shooting at your buddies. In many cases, you're wearing camouflage too. Beware: Getting hit with a paintball does hurt. The paint flies at 280 feet per second, so wear layers of clothing, tie a scarf around your neck, and wear a cup. Or say hello to some nice new bruises.

Sample Scenarios

The Pocono Paintball Company (800-876-0285), in Jim Thorpe, PA, offers a bachelor party package in which the bachelor plays for free with a group of fifteen; the best man is free, too, if your group size is over thirty. If you have at least fifteen players, you qualify for a private field with your own referees. They have twenty-two fields; 150 acres of paintball and 20 acres dedicated to other activities (like baseball and picnics).

Approximate Cost per Person? Plan for $50 to $75 per person for six hours of play (includes camouflage, paint, goggles, field admission, gun, mask, and CO_2 for the day).

How Far in Advance Should You Plan? Three weeks is a healthy minimum.

Number of Days for Event? One.

Photo or Video Ops? Bring your own camera and capture your friends' sadistic glee—and their colorful injuries.

Booze Policy? Allowed only at the end of the day. Never on the field.

SKYDIVING/BUNGEE JUMPING

No one really knows how safe this is, but there are plenty of companies around to help you fall off planes and bridges and cranes. Surprisingly, training often involves less than an hour of watching videos and going over procedures. Regardless of the risk factor, there's nothing like staring death in the face. If you attend one of the bachelor parties, you'll inevitably hear someone invoke the lame metaphor that taking this kind of dive doesn't compare to diving into marriage. He may have a point.

Sample Scenarios

At Skydive California City (888-373-4007/*www.skydivecalifor niacity.com*), there are two skydiving courses available:

1. Tandem diving with ½-hour training (free falling 15,000 feet above sea level for forty to fifty seconds, followed by parachute falling of six minutes or so). Costs $199 per person (six or more, $189; ten or more, $179).
2. Accelerated free fall, in which you free fall with two instructors on either side of you. This requires seven hours of training. Costs $299 per person. Photos or video costs $60 ($75 for both). Parties may sleep on the premises (camp on grass or in camper) and use the private swimming pool and showers. A barbecue is also available for free. Must be over eighteen and weigh less than 225 pounds.

At Sky's the Limit Skydiving Center (800-335-JUMP/*www.skys thelimit.net*) in Newton, New Jersey, your first jump will be from up at 13,500 feet. The prices are as follows:

Tandem Skydive Weekday (May 1–October 31): $165
Tandem Skydive Weekend (May 1–October 31): $180
Tandem Skydive (November 1–April 31): $199
Video Package—$85 plus tax

If you have a group of eleven, the organizer can jump free or they'll take $10 off everyone's jump. Camping and hotels are approximately five minutes away.

Bungee jumping at Bungee Experience in California (209-295-6123/*www.californiabungee.com*) in Pioneer, CA, costs $50 per person for one jump or $90 for two.

Approximate Cost per Person? Bungee jumping costs $50 to $100 per person and skydiving costs between $150 and $300 per person.

How Far in Advance Should You Plan? Two weeks minimum.

Number of Days for Event? One or two days.

Photo or Video Ops? The classic shot captures the groom's look of terror as he plunges thousands of feet. Take your own shots or pay extra for a (sometimes professionally edited) video.

Booze Policy? No beer in the plane or while diving. It's never a good idea to drink and dive.

MAJOR LEAGUE BASEBALL GAME

What could be more American than chugging beers at the game? Everyone likes baseball, and there's a seat for every budget—from bleachers to private rooms. At some stadiums, you can get a message flashed on the scoreboard (such as "Cubs congratulate bachelor John Doe") or even an on-air greeting from the play-by-play man (which you'll be able to hear on your private TVs). Ask the guy who rents you the skybox how to do it. And if you don't have the cash? Bleacher seats and beer make most men happy—and that's as cheap as any party gets. Just make sure you secure seats in advance; sometimes it's hard to find space for twenty guys in the same area. One last idea: Make it a field trip to as many ballgames at as many ballparks as you can pack into a weekend.

Sample Scenarios

Boston Red Sox: After the game, if you want to gawk in a meat-market environment, hit the Big Easy or any other club in the Boylston Place Alleyway. If you want to look at gals gyrate to techno music, head over to Avalon, Bill's Bar, or any other club on Lansdowne Street—all are near Fenway Park and Jillian's pool hall. Sox tix cost between $18 and $60 per person. Call the club's group sales department for bachelor party ideas and discounts.

Chicago Cubs: You can get a seat at Wrigley Field for between $12 and $36. Mezzanine suites cost between $1,500 and $7,200, but include indoor and outdoor seating, climate control, TVs— and a killer view of the action. Order a food package ahead or go à la carte. Since boxes open two hours before game time and close an hour after, you can beat traffic and get your money's worth. Alternatively, you could kill an entire day walking around Wrigley too. Within easy walking distance, there's everything from cheap bar food to high-end French restaurants. Good bars include Cubby Bear (at Clark and Addison) and Murphy's Bleachers (across the street from the entrance to Wrigley's bleachers). In fact, if your group is big enough, you can enjoy the game on top of a roof deck next to Murphy's (they own it) for a fee that ranges from $2,500 to $5,000, including all beverages and food.

New York Yankees: It doesn't get rowdier than in the bleacher section at Yankee Stadium in the Bronx. Thank God for the bleacher creatures (usually in section 39)—those rabid fans who scream at opposing teams, chant like drunken frat boys at the top of their lungs, and demand attention from Yankee players every game. Better yet, prices for bleacher seats are $8.00 and it's just a subway ride outta Manhattan.

Arizona Diamondbacks: They won the series in 2001, and they have a helluva stadium (Bank One Ballpark) to boot. Infiniti Diamond Level Luxury Suites are equipped with a private temperature-controlled indoor lounge, TV, private rest room, refrigerator, and icemaker. They accommodate eighteen to thirty-six people, with prices starting at $1,350 per game. Not good enough? Try the Party Suites located in right field, with outdoor balcony seating, a private temperature-controlled indoor lounge, high-top tables and chairs, bar, and TVs. Holds groups of 24 to 254 with prices starting at $1,800 per game. Better still is the Sun Pool Party Pavilion located in right-centerfield, with a 385-square-foot pool (!), an 85-square-foot spa, and a patio area. Locker rooms and shower facilities are also part of the Pavilion; the pool accommodates thirty-five people and is priced at $5,000 per game. Too much? There are always the deep foul line seats for just $6.00.

Approximate Cost per Person? For the budget-impaired, it's generally $10 and up for no-frills bleacher seats and a beer. If you have the cash, you can spend hundreds or thousands on box seats. Don't forget to factor in food and drink. Parking is usually cheap—and preferred parking often comes with the big group bookings.

How Far in Advance Should You Plan? It varies, but at some ballparks you need to start calling in late February. Several months are often necessary.

Number of Days for Event? One.

Photo or Video Ops? The scoreboard flashing your buddy's name.

Booze Policy? Ever been to a ballpark before? Just make sure you drink early on since some parks stop serving during the seventh inning.

Dude Ranch/Hunting/Riflery

What other activity has the word "dude" in it? And dude ranches offer something for everyone—nature, sports, shooting stuff. Most dude ranches are rustic hotels, located on a large plot of rural land. They offer any and all of the following: horseback, archery, riflery, camping, fishing, rafting, and hiking. More plush

"Well, what do you expect for ten cents a dance?"

resorts may also host golf and tennis. Fresh gourmet meals are often par for the course.

Sample Scenarios

If you're searching for your own inner predator, consider a dude ranch that offers no-kidding-around hunting. Drive eighty miles east of Atlanta, for example, and you'll find Durhamtown Plantation Sportsman's Resort (706-486-4603/*www.durhamtown .com*)—with 5,700 acres of manly activities. Hunting packages go for $225 per person, per day, and include three meals and deluxe lodging in a two-room cabin that sleeps up to four people. Guests may hunt small game, like quail, rabbit, squirrel, and dove, or large game, like deer and hog. A three-day package on the larger game runs $575 per person. All hunts are booked by reservation so guides can take hunters into and out of the hunting areas. The resort is always open, but the hunts are, of course, seasonal. Those less inclined to shoot animals can shoot sporting clays (or play paintball). Horseback alone costs $60 for a full day; ATVs (all-terrain vehicles) cost $90 per day. Less expensive lodging options include bunks for $10 a person and cabins for $25 a night.

Approximate Cost per Person? Depends on how luxurious the lodging is, what activities you choose, and when you go. While fishing trips are often inexpensive ($100 for a guide), hunting packages can cost thousands, though that covers a full week of sport. Expect $1,000 to $1,500 per person per week at a dude ranch—including meals, horseback riding, and lodging (some places require a full week's stay during peak season). Winter season rates are much cheaper and you may not have to spend a whole week there.

How Far in Advance Should You Plan? Several months if it's a big party.

Number of Days for Event? Plan for at least a weekend.

Photo or Video Ops? Take snapshots of the groom in camouflage, holding a rifle or on a horse.

Booze Policy? Guns and booze don't mix. So wait till dark . . . to drink, that is.

SKIING/SNOWBOARDING

You can tell a lot about people by watching whether they grab skis or a snowboard. While the tension between the groups has died down since the early days of snowboarding, there's still some sense that snowboarders are young, rascally ruffians and the skiers are stuffy snobs. No matter what you choose, you'll have to pay for a lift pass to allow you access to the mountain and ski lift, plus equipment, meals, and lodging (and lessons for those who've never done this before). The more you bring the more you save. Groups of twenty to twenty-five or more often get discounts. Plan on sharing rooms.

Sample Scenarios

Mammoth Mountain: Located in the Eastern Sierras, four hours north of L.A., Mammoth Mountain (800-MAMMOTH/*www. mammothmountain.com*) is a winter sports Mecca. It's generally open November through July. Lift tickets cost $56 a day for a one-day pass and $107 for a two-day pass (five bucks off a two-day pass if you're a group of more than twenty-five and the twenty-sixth ticket is free). Ski packages cost $26 per person and include boots, skis, and poles; the equivalent snowboard package costs $30.

Stowe Mountain Resort: On the other coast—in Vermont—you can buy a one-day pass for $58 or a two-day pass for $97. Ski and snowboard packages cost $28 a day. Group packages are available too: 20 or more people are considered a group; the twenty-first gets free lodging, lift tickets, and meal packages (all if pre-arranged).

Approximate Cost per Person?
One-day pass: $60
Two-day pass: $100
Equipment rental: $30 per day
Lodging, food, and pot are extra.
How Far in Advance Should You Plan? One month minimum.
Number of Days for Event? One or two.
Photo or Video Ops? Cameras can capture the groom jumping, slaloming, or falling down a mountain. Better yet, catch a group photo with some ski bunnies back at the lodge. . . .
Booze Policy? Drink at the ski lodge at the end of the day. Expect the fresh mountain air to bring out the smokers too.

CAR RACING/BUMPER CARS/TANKS

There are two types of car freaks: speed demons and demolition derby drivers. If you want to experience acceleration beyond 100 mph, you'll have to sign up for a track lesson. Members of the bachelor party will inevitably compete to see who hits top speed. And that usually means 145 to 150 mph. If you prefer collisions and crashes, consider the many bumper car tracks—the only places where drinking and driving is okay.

Sample Scenarios
The college town of Ann Arbor—45 miles southwest of Detroit—is where automobiles have been melded with basketball, polo, and hockey to form a new, inexpensive game known as Whirly Ball. Two teams of five square off against each another in

electric bumper cars known as Whirly Bugs. Armed with plastic scoops, each team tries to throw a whiffle ball the size of a grapefruit into the opponent's fifteen-inch net, which stands at each end of a 4,000-square-foot metal court. Each game lasts about thirty minutes. There's some sweating, some bumping, and plenty of opportunities to let loose the road warrior that dwells within us all. Bring your own food and roll in your favorite kegs of brew. Don't worry, there are no speed traps or cops on the court. Cost is just $125 Monday through Thursday and $145 Friday through Sunday—and that's based on an hourly rental (not per person). Half of the price must be paid when making the reservation. For more information call 734-975-6909 after 1 P.M. There are two courts available for rental. Shoot the groom, beer in hand, driving with that malicious, competitive grin. Drink and drive? You bet!

From the same state, with a different concept, is TrackTime Driving School (866-2-DRIVE-1/*www.tracktime.com*), a place that's right next to Michigan International Speedway and offers half-day and one-day courses in stock cars and high-performance cars like BMW Z35 and Formula 3 cars. The fun begins with a classroom introduction to the dynamics of driving, moves on to the track with instructors, and then heads back into the classroom. From here on, you drive solo. Half-day participants receive two six-lap sessions in the stock cars. Full-day participants receive four six-lap sessions. Classes run May through end of September.

With all the recent U.S. patriotism, there is no doubt interest in all things military. At the Tactical Tanks facility in Sherman, Texas (903-893-2129/*www.tacticaltanks.com*), bachelor party members can engage in mock combat using real tanks. You'll be driving tanks from the United States and the United Kingdom—without weapons—somewhere on the company's 150 acres of land (sixty-five miles north of Dallas). The driving itself takes between ten and forty-five minutes, come rain or shine. Just imagine the photo opportunities.

Approximate Cost per Person?
TrackTime Driving School
Ten or more get the discount as follows:
One half day: $545 per person
One full day: $895 per person

Whirly Ball
Figure on $125 to $145 per group.

Tactical Tanks
Plan on $450 to $2,500 per person and up, depending on how many people want to drive tanks, what tanks you want to drive, and whether you want lunch, photos, dog tags, patches, videos, and other extras.

How Far in Advance Should You Plan? Thirty days minimum is advised. Weekend nights are booked farthest in advance.

Number of Days for Event? One day; hotels are nearby so it could stretch into a weekend.

Photo or Video Ops? Catch the groom emerging victorious from the car/tank or at least wearing a helmet/uniform.

Booze Policy? Don't drink and drive—unless you're driving bumper cars.

TOURNAMENTS: TENNIS/BASKETBALL/BASEBALL/FOOTBALL/ SOCCER/VOLLEYBALL

Too many outdoorsy/athletic activities tap your budget as much as your stamina (think: paintball). Not so with tennis, baseball, football, soccer, volleyball, or basketball. All you need is a court/ diamond/field and the requisite equipment. If you have fewer than twenty guys, you can rent a professional-sized court like the basketball court at Chicago's Lakeshore Athletic Center, which charges up to $300 per hour, depending on when you need it. Michael Jordan has been known to drop in for a pickup game, but don't count on it.

If you have more than twenty guys, you might want to create a round robin tournament in which there are two or three rounds of competition. Or see who can throw the farthest, hit the longest, or kick the highest. Dole out prizes for the winners (beer, sex props, gift certificates).

The Advantages of a Sports-oriented Party Include:

- Low cost (unless you rent that pro basketball court)
- Flexible timing—no need to "get there on time" or leave after a certain hour
- Easy access; find a park or a court
- Beer is allowed and is cheaper than if you paid for catering
- Non-sportsmen can build a BBQ or play Frisbee or just drink if they so choose
- Can be thrown together last-minute—as a plan B perhaps

Disadvantages:

- It sounds like a plan B.

Approximate Cost per Person? From zilch to $100 per person, if you include food, booze, and possible hourly fee for the facility.

How Far in Advance Should You Plan? Could be as late as that morning if you've already assembled all the guests.

Number of Days for Event? One day of running around is plenty.

Photo or Video Ops? Bonus points if you catch the groom stumbling, making funny faces, or passed out on the grass.

Booze Policy? Bring it on.

Swanky Activities

If you've got money to spare—or a snobby crowd to please—consider a swanky night out with the boys. This is ideal for nonathletic types who appreciate the finer things in life like gourmet food, fine wine, cigars, Scotch, and massages. They want luxuries. They want to treat themselves. In some cases, they can have all of the above. What better excuse to splurge than to celebrate your buddy's last night as a single man?

GAMBLING AT CASINOS

Everyone wants to get something for nothing, even if it costs hundreds. That's the lure of gambling. It doesn't matter what your game is—poker, blackjack, roulette, slots—for a while, at least, you'll be up. Buy a few $100 chips for the groom (you can pool all the guys' money to do this) and he can play like a high roller . . . for a little while.

Casinos make it very comfortable indeed. The crafty folks who own these places may or may not pump oxygen into the rooms to keep you happy but they certainly hire attractive waitresses to serve cocktails (for free) and keep the joints open twenty-four

"But I am wearing a mask."

hours a day. Your animal instincts take over and *voilà,* you're craving the big payout. Stick cigars in your mouths and you feel like winners even if you lose. I suggest you bring cash only; you don't want your bank/credit cards to tempt you as you lean drunkenly on the cash-dispensing machine at 3 A.M. Also beware of the cute girls hanging on your arms, especially in Nevada.

Finally, here's some advice for real high rollers: Don't keep wads of cash in your wallet to pay tips; buy several denominations of poker chips—anywhere from $50 to $5,000, for example—and dole them out like candy.

Best and Worst Odds

Best (Assuming You Use Some Strategy)

- Blackjack
- Craps
- Pai Gow Poker
- Baccarat
- Roulette
- Video Poker (full pay machines)
- Sic Bo
- Slots (at high payout casinos)

Worst

- Keno
- Let It Ride
- Caribbean Stud Poker
- Red Dog
- Big Six Wheel

Sample Scenarios

Las Vegas, Nevada: Everything's here: girls, glamour, gambling. Not to mention museums (like the Guggenheim at the Venetian), discos (like Studio 54 at the MGM Grand), and a burgeoning gastronomic scene—Vegas is restaurant central nowadays. On the strip, you'll find dozens of major-name casinos, each luring you in with a distinct theme. The swankiest are Caesar's Palace, the Venetian, and the Bellagio. These are gigantic shrines to gambling with thousands of rooms, tables, slot machines, celebrity chef restaurants, glitzy bars, indoor shopping malls, luxurious swimming pools and spas. The Hard Rock Hotel has by far the youngest— and sexiest—crowd with a bustling singles scene on weekend nights. You really can't go wrong since all casinos have poker, blackjack, roulette, craps, and slot machines. See also the chapter on "Hot Spots" for Las Vegas.

Reno, Nevada: Known as "The Biggest Little City in the World," Reno feels like the Old West. It's gruffer than Vegas (which is now like Disneyland). It's sleazier. It seems meaner. But for some people, that's the real deal. The city is divided into two areas: "downtown" and everywhere else. Downtown is more tightly packed, with a dense array of casinos and hotels. The outlying areas are more spread out, prettier, offer better parking, and may be safer. Popular casinos include Atlantis, Boomtown, Comstock, Eldorado, Harrah's Hotel Casino, Monarch, Peppermill, Reno Hilton, Sands, Siena, and the Silver Legacy Resort Casino. Reno is also near Carson City and Lake Tahoe (which has its own activities and gambling). Vegas is several hours south.

Atlantic City, New Jersey: Atlantic City is one hour away by car from Philly, two hours away from New York, and just thirty hours from Dallas (oh well). There are twelve casinos, bright sandy beaches, a four and a half mile amusement-filled boardwalk, championship golf courses, tennis, charter boat fishing, sailing, restaurants, and plenty of bars. You can have the limo take you or you can consider inexpensive (and sometimes free) public transportation from nearby cities. With more than 33 million people visiting every year, this is the East Coast's Vegas, though far more sleazy and scaled back.

Ledyard, Connecticut: Who knew that the "world's biggest casino and resort complex" was in Connecticut? It's called Foxwoods Resort and Casino (800-FOXWOODS/*www.foxwoods.com*), and it's reasonably near Boston, Hartford, Providence, and New York. Built on a Pequot Indian reservation, Foxwood boasts 6,400 slot machines, 350 table games, 6 casinos, and the world's largest bingo hall (okay, maybe that's not so cool for bachelor parties). It's got the usual hotels and restaurants with free drinks at the big tables and championship golf courses located nearby. As at most casinos, there's something going on 24/7. You'll find other casinos throughout the U.S.A., many on reservations or boats—and not just on the coasts either. In the Midwest and South, this includes:

Biloxi, Mississippi: Grand Casino Biloxi
Gulfport, Mississippi: Grand Casino Gulfport
Tunica, Michigan: Bally's
New Orleans, Los Angeles: Bally's, Harrah's
New Albany, Indiana (across the river from Louisville):
     Caesar's

Approximate Cost per Person? Count on gambling away $100 a day and up. Any less and you might as well go to Disneyland. Hotel rooms cost between $75 and $500 depending upon the type of room, season, and availability. Ask about group discounts and try to book all of your rooms on the same floor.

How Far in Advance Should You Plan? Several weeks, ideally. Avoid peak seasons (like major holidays) and find out if any conventions will be in the area since that can destroy your chances of getting hotel rooms.

Number of Days for Event? Two days.

Photo or Video Ops? Find out if the casino allows it first. Then snap a shot of the groom at the poker table, slots, and roulette wheel—or of him holding a wad of cash at the start of the night and emptying his pockets by the end of the night.

Booze Policy? They'll bring it for free if you gamble enough. They want you drunk.

MASSAGE/SPA TREATMENTS

Don't laugh. This is an increasingly popular activity for men who want to live the good life. It's a trend brought about by the growth in men's beauty products (not that you could tell) and the growing sentiment that it's okay to pamper yourself. Chances are, if you scoff at facials, massages, and manicures, you've never tried them.

Most resorts and better hotels offer some kind of spa treatment, but some are renowned for their facilities, staff, and picturesque surroundings. The party becomes a whole weekend of decadence: champagne, caviar, limos, fine dining, and so on (sounds like a hip-hop video, huh?). The Four Seasons Hotels have made it an art. This has spurred on other hotels—especially in Las Vegas—to

tip: Make sure you understand what kind of massage you've signed on for since some are rougher than others. They'll be glad to explain the options. Offer a tip if you enjoyed it.

up the luxury quotient in recent years. It's not just about luring men with loose slots and cheap food. Or was that loose women and cheap slots? Anyway, hotels have found that if they flaunt great workout facilities or professional aromatherapy spas, a high-paid clientele will come running. Just say no to female mud wrestling and yes to mud baths.

Better spas offer some or all of the following services:

- **Aromatherapy** (yes, you can treat psychological and physical ailments by smelling the right oils)
- **Massage** (find out what you're getting—Swedish, shiatsu, deep tissue, reflexology, etc.—and how it works before you make the appointment)
- **Manicure** (women notice things like hands and fingernails, so you might want to clean them up)
- **Pedicure** (if you're working the pool area for a date, splurge for one of these too)
- **Facial** (not foreign women popping your pimples; technicians also apply various masks and exfoliation techniques to make your skin glow)
- **Steam Bath/Sauna** (rarely coed, but thoroughly relaxing, pore cleansing, and full of male-bonding conversations . . . don't spend more than fifteen minutes in here, though)
- **Workout facilities** (gyms, rock-climbing walls, pools)
- **Nutrition consultation** (this can shape your body far faster than a zillion bench presses and squats)

All you have to do is book an appointment, ideally well in advance. Wear whatever you like; the spa usually provides a robe, slippers, and a locker for your belongings. Arrive early and shower beforehand if you can. If you're having a facial, shave a few hours earlier—not just before you arrive. You can request a male

> *tip:* If you want to coordinate a bachelor and bachelorette party at the same time and place, consider a spa or resort.

or female masseuse, though it hardly matters since a towel covers your private parts.

Sample Scenarios

Venetian, Las Vegas, Nevada: The Canyon Ranch SpaClub (877-220-2688/*www.canyonranch.com*) is a world-famous luxury getaway. At the Vegas outpost, they offer acupuncture, massages (shiatsu and other variations), reflexology, and some truly exotic, ancient treatments like the $160 "Rasul Ceremony" (Middle Eastern ritual of medicinal mud, steam, herbs, rain shower in a steam chamber) and $185 "Abhyanga" (two therapists massage you simultaneously with sesame oil)—among many others. Rates are slightly higher Friday through Monday.

Four Seasons, Las Vegas, Nevada: The technicians at the Four Seasons Spa (702-632-5000/*www.fourseasons.com/lasvegas/vacations/spa_services.html*) have developed a special "gentlemen's facial" for masculine skin that involves skin analysis, exfoliation, a replenishing mask, and facial massage. A fifty-minute session (massage or facial) costs $115; eighty minutes costs $175. Other exotic body care treatments include a Seaweed Body Mask, Bali Spice Scrub, and Champagne Mud Wrap—each for $110 to $135.

Two Bunch Palms, Desert Hot Springs, California: Legend has it that Al Capone spent time here (800-472-4334/*www.twobunch palms.com*) and built up a fortress that became the playground for Mafia bosses and movie stars, replete with stone bungalows, stained-glass windows, rock fireplaces, spa, and casino. Now it's a retro-bohemian, natural hot springs resort, with a variety of spa treatments and fine dining options—all very tranquil (so don't come here to party). Of note is the spectacular grotto (matched only by the one in the Playboy Mansion), which supposedly confers restorative and medicinal results on those who bathe in its hot natural mineral waters. One-hour sessions—massages, facials, mud treatments—generally cost $90 while 1.5 hours costs $130 to $140.

Approximate Cost per Person? Plan for $85 and up per person, per hour, minimum.

How Far in Advance Should You Plan? Months, if you want to book a block of rooms on the same floor.

Number of Days for Event? Two days.

Photo or Video Ops? You could potentially capture the groom reclining, Hef-style, in a satin robe with pipe dangling from mouth and a glass of Scotch on the rocks in his hand. Or consider the shot of him being rubbed down by some strong-handed hottie.

Booze Policy? Michelob and massage don't mix.

RESORT WEEKEND

Resorts give you the best of all possible worlds: luxurious accommodations, modern amenities, access to sports and the outdoors, and the option to back out at any time if one of the party members is not up for the group scene. Plan a resort weekend and you can add any of the other activities listed in this book—golf, skiing, tennis, scuba diving, wine tasting, spa treatments, gambling, fishing, sailing—or more than one. Taking it one step farther, you can pay the club pro for tennis or golf or skiing lessons.

First, think about climate and activities—beach or snowy mountains? Next, decide if you want to stay in or near a city or in the country. Then consider local versus faraway destinations (travel fares can add up). Finally, look at price ranges.

Sample Scenarios

The Broadmoor, Colorado Springs, Colorado: Located at the foot of the Rockies and surrounded by the mountains, the Broadmoor (800-634-7711/*www.broadmoor.com*) boasts three thousand acres surrounding Cheyenne Lake. It's one of the few resorts in the country to have earned the Mobil Five Star and the AAA Five Diamond ratings every year since the awards were established. And it's got real history: Born in 1891 as a gambling casino, it was transformed into a true resort in 1918. Guests can play golf or tennis in pro-level facilities and/or indulge in spa treatments, bicycling, horseback riding, and ballooning. Special half-day and all-day fly-fishing programs are available for about $115 a person (you'll find rainbow, brown, and cutthroat trout in the South Platte River).

The Hotel Del Coronado, near San Diego, California: Here's a national landmark, historical treasure, and thoroughly modern and ambitious resort packed with possibilities for bachelor parties. The hotel (800-HOTELDEL/*www.hoteldel.com*) was built on twenty-six beachfront acres in 1888 and has seen many a celebrity guest, including every U.S. president since Benjamin Harrison (in 1891), Frank Sinatra, and Marilyn Monroe, who starred in *Some Like It Hot*—shot on location at the Del in 1958. Of course, there's the usual laundry list of activities: golf, tennis, swimming, spa treatments, and boating (sailboats, speedboats, water skis, jet skis, paddleboats, and kayaks). The golf courses and boating facilities are located off the hotel's premises at nearby facilities.

Approximate Cost per Person?
Broadmoor

Rooms alone range from $230 per room a night to $3,170 for their best suite.

Golf: $193 and up (based on double occupancy), per person (includes room, personal locker, range balls, greens fee, and cart rental).

Tennis: $25 to $30 an hour for a court; $150 for private instructor (or $50 per person to play a doubles match against the pros—if you win, it's free!).

Fly-fishing: $115 and up, per person.

Room, spa access, and massage: $186 and up, per person.

Hotel Del Coronado

Rooms alone range from $250 to $2,300 a room per night.

Golf: $38 to $225 per person (courses nearby but not on the premises; cart included; reservation fee may be extra).

Tennis: Free to guests.

Boating: Call the nearby boathouse (619-437-1514) for rates.

How Far in Advance Should You Plan? Months and months if you want rooms together, access to tennis courts and golf courses, and/or plan on visiting during peak seasons.

Number of Days for Event? Two.

Photo or Video Ops? Playing golf, getting a massage, swimming in the pool.

Booze Policy? Rich people know how to drink. Join them.

STEAK (AND CIGARS)

Steaks represent a primal indulgence thoroughly appropriate for bachelor parties. Maybe it's because we're ripping into the flesh of thick, juicy hunks of meat with glorious abandon—just as our ancestors did centuries ago. Or maybe it just tastes so damn good.

You can host any kind of party by day and by night, as long as you have a steak dinner to refuel. Pick a decent steakhouse—and every city has a few—and you have an instant party, during which time the group can talk shit, drink Scotch, maybe smoke cigars, and debate the merits of different cuts of steak. You'd better come prepared. Here are some meaty guidelines.

Steak Tips

- "Black and blue" means rare on the inside and charred on the outside. Most chefs recommend you order a steak medium-rare. If you order well done, you're asking the chef to cook the flavor out of the meat. Your choice.
- Learn the difference between porterhouse, sirloin, filet mignon, and other cuts. Go to a grocery store, butcher, or restaurant and look at how large, fatty, and thick each cut is.
- The best steaks have thin streaks of fat known as marbling. This adds to the flavor. Too little fat and your steak won't be as tasty. Too much fat and the steak will be tough. So it's a balancing act to find a steak that's tasty and tender. Filet mignon tends to be tender, but not as flavorful as a rib eye and sirloin.
- The porterhouse is a giant slab o' beef that consists of three parts: tenderloin (the most tender cut of beef, which, if served separately, is called filet mignon), bone, and another, triangular section of meat. When served separately, this triangular section is called New York steak—also called New York strip steak, Delmonico steak, and shell steak.
- Order the spinach. You should have something green on your plate.
- Order a "loaf" of onion rings, if available. Looks like a brick. Feeds an army.

Read more about beef here: *www.beef.org/documents//BME_ chart.pdf.*

Best Steakhouses (According to Zagat Guides)

Atlanta
Chops
Bone's
Ruth's Chris Steak House
Prime
McKendrick's Steakhouse

Boston
Morton's of Chicago
Grill 23 & Bar
Oak Room
Capital Grille
Abe & Louie's

Chicago
Morton's of Chicago
Gibsons Steakhouse
Chicago Chop House
Ruth's Chris Steak House
Capital Grille

Dallas/Fort Worth
Del Frisco's Double Eagle Steak House
Bob's Steak & Chop House
Pappas Bros. Steakhouse
Chamberlain's
Capital Grille

Las Vegas

Prime Steakhouse
Morton's of Chicago
Delmonico
The Steak House
Charlie Palmer Steak

Los Angeles

Ruth's Chris Steak House
Arnie Morton's of Chicago
Lawry's the Prime Rib
Palm
Arroyo Chop House
The Grill

Miami

Palm
Morton's of Chicago
Ruth's Chris Steakhouse
The Forge
Capital Grille

Minneapolis/St. Paul

Manny's Steakhouse
Ruth's Chris Steak House
Morton's of Chicago
Murray's
Lindey's Prime Steak House

New Orleans

Ruth's Chris Steak House
Rib Room

Young's
Dickie Brennan's Steakhouse
Steak Knife Restaurant & Bar

New York
Peter Luger Steak House
Sparks Steak House
Palm
Morton's of Chicago
Post House
Smith & Wollensky

Philadelphia
Prime Rib
Morton's of Chicago
Palm
Sullivan's Steakhouse
Kansas City Prime

San Francisco
Cole's Chop House
Vic Stewart's
Morton's of Chicago
House of Prime Rib
Harris'

Seattle
Metropolitan Grill
Jak's Grill
Ruth's Chris Steak House
Daniel's Broiler
Fleming's Prime Steakhouse & Wine Bar

Washington, D.C.
Prime Rib

Morton's of Chicago

Ruth's Chris Steak House

Palm

Sam & Harry's

Cigars
See "Cigars 101" on page 34 for information about what to buy, how to cut, and how to light.

Approximate Cost per Person? Plan on $100 for the steak dinner (includes a drink or two) and $20 for a cigar—per person.

How Far in Advance Should You Plan? A few weeks gives you more than enough time.

Number of Days for Event? One night.

Photo or Video Ops? The groom standing with the Mafioso-looking host, the groom about to dive into a thick steak, the groom plugging away at a cigar surrounded by buddies.

Booze Policy? Scotch goes well with cigars. Wait until after you're done with the steaks.

CRUISE

If you're looking for an outdoorsy, mellow, picturesque, and nonathletic activity, consider a cruise. There are all kinds: day trips, night trips, weekend, and week-long trips. You can charter your own or join a huge sailing vessel with the hopes of meeting a pack of girls. But like a fishing expedition (see "Fishing" page 56), it is only as good as the organizer makes it. Better ones will have great eats, unlimited booze, indoor and outdoor seating, and perhaps a few stops along the way at piers and docks.

Sample Scenarios

In Maryland, cruise-goers gravitate to the Inner Harbor area of downtown Baltimore for water cruises through the Chesapeake Bay south to Annapolis or north to Aberdeen. More interesting is "crabbing," a time-honored tradition that's half sport and half seafood quest. Catching crabs isn't difficult (insert stripper joke here). You simply tie a chicken bone to a string, toss the bone into the bay, and wait for one of the critters to make a suicidal grasp. Once those babies have hold of the bone, they're not letting go—until you haul them on deck and make them.

Once the catch is on board, head north to Aberdeen or south to Annapolis, where caterers can meet you and provide small tables and linen tablecloths to complement a celebratory dinner. Don't worry about how full a feast you'll haul in. Caterers will be glad to bring their own food to fix for you—just in case you've sworn off ever catching crabs again.

In Boston, the Bay State Cruise Line (617-748-1428/*www.bay statecruisecompany.com*) offers an Entertainment Cruise (aka Booze Cruise) each Friday and Saturday night where groups of party-goers load the *Provincetown II* (capacity 1,100) and chug around the Boston Harbor and outer islands. The per-person fee is $16 to $20, with a DJ or live music, and there's a cash bar. It's a popular destination for bachelor and bachelorette parties. The boat leaves Commonwealth Pier at 8:30 P.M. and returns at 11:30 P.M.

In Washington D.C., bachelor parties may boat down the Potomac River, which provides the best view in town—from the Old Town Alexandria and National Airport to the illuminated Capitol dome and monuments. Boats can dock near Georgetown or Old Town in Alexandria. You can have dinner in town, cruise the bars, or generally carouse with the groom-to-be. One boat in particular, *The Irish Mist* (202-488-7007), caters to bachelor parties and costs $250 per hour. There is a two-hour minimum and a $50 charge for docking. The yacht sails from the Southwest Washington Harbor. Catering prices vary; plan on up to $70 to $80 per person, depending on how much you eat and drink.

Approximate Cost per Person? Depends on the size of the boat and catering, but generally $25 to $75 per person.

How Far in Advance Should You Plan? Two weeks or more.

Number of Days for Event? One.

Photo or Video Ops? Bachelor on the top level, wind blowing through his hair (and maybe blowing his hat off), looking like he's freezing or drunk or both. Scenic monuments in the background.

Booze Policy? Ask your captain before boarding.

GAMBLING AT THE HORSE TRACK

The allure of horseracing has captivated the souls of betting men for thousands of years. "The sport of kings" has become one of those rare pastimes that cross age, race, and class lines. But how do you host a bachelor party at the track?

First, you give your group the full VIP treatment. Most horse tracks have an upscale eatery, located on the penthouse level overlooking the skyline and featuring a stunning interior of perhaps leather, marble, or brass.

But the primary goal, of course, is to win cash. That said, at the start of the first race the guys could each chip in a couple of bucks for the groom, placing one large bet or, perhaps, a different friend can place a small bet at the start of each race. After winning a couple of bucks of honeymoon spending dough, the groom will soon forget any stripper action he might be missing. For those who may not feel comfortable at the betting cage, the track offers prepaid betting vouchers as well as free handicapping seminars.

As with most party halls, a 25 percent deposit is required to confirm your group's arrangements. Final payment is required two weeks before the function. Most of the track packages include admission, racing program, and a cordial welcome on the Sony Jumbotron and on in-house monitors. Remember that proper attire is a must, so wear only the best in sport jackets and collared shirts—no jeans and no sneakers. Minimum group size is usually around twenty.

Sample Scenario

At Belmont Park in New York (516-488-6000/*www.nyracing. com/Belmont*), bachelor parties have a number of group sales options. First, you can reserve brunch, lunch, or buffet at the Garden Terrace, a trackside restaurant with panoramic views of the racing. This includes choice of appetizer, main course, clubhouse admission, and a program guide. Minimum is twenty-five people at around $26 a pop. You can also ask for an open bar for four hours (for about $25 a person) or ask for more private rooms, including the executive box with private wagering, closed-circuit TV, and a view overlooking the finish line (at $38 per person).

To personalize the event, ask a group salesperson if a race can be named in honor of the bachelor. Even better, you can pay $125 and give four guests the honor of presenting a trophy to the winning owner or owner's representative. The moment will be captured in a commemorative photo. Or splurge another $125 to get the whole party down to the paddock to view the saddling of the horse and mounting of the jockey.

Approximate Cost per Person?

Small Budget: As little as $1.50 to $5.00 admission without an all-inclusive luxury party.

Big Budget: $40 to $60 per person, depending on food selections, seating, and other amenities.

How Far in Advance Should You Plan? At least two weeks, but book early.

Number of Days for the Event? One.

Photo or Video Ops? The groom (with three buddies) can stand in the winner's circle with the jockey, owner, and trainer (this can cost $125 or more, so ask in advance).

Booze Policy? Drink Mint Juleps, Kentucky Derby–style at the bar.

HIRING CELEBRITY LOOK-ALIKES

The groom loves Pamela Anderson. She won't come to his party. But an impersonator will. Don't tell the groom that the (other) love of his life is showing up; just let it happen. If he's a golf fanatic, send Tiger Woods to the golf course while you're there and rig it so the groom and Tiger happen upon a situation in which they must exchange a few words. Or go paint the town with Elvis. Maybe the groom's a politics junkie. Or a film buff. Or a Trekkie. Doesn't matter. If you hire a celebrity look-alike to join you in public, you're bound to attract attention. Hire a male movie star and you'll find out what happens when you hang out with chick magnets like Brad Pitt or Mel Gibson. Go to sites like *www.epic1.com/entertainment/lookalike/lookalikes.html* and *www.lookalikes-usa.com,* and you can search by celebrity name and look at photos of many of the star look-alikes. Or ask them to send you a video. I was floored by the realism in the photos of Marilyn Monroe, Seinfeld's Kramer, Louis Armstrong, Madonna, O.J. Simpson, Britney Spears, and Tiger Woods. Look for a company that offers this kind of service in your city. In Britain, check out *www.entertainmentuk.com.*

Approximate Cost per Person? Depends on who you want, how far he or she has to drive or fly, and how long you want the look-alike to stay. Rates start at $250 per hour and go up to $1,000 per hour.

How Far in Advance Should You Plan? One month so you get the celeb you really want—and he or she has time to come to your city. You may be able to find someone in twenty-four hours too, but that's a gamble.

Number of Days for the Event? One.

Photo or Video Ops? The groom standing next to the celeb, maybe even getting physical with her.

Booze Policy? The drunker you are, the more they'll look like the real thing.

Inexpensive Activities

Don't be embarrassed or ashamed by low-budget activities. These can be even more fun than sporty or swanky events because the expectations are generally low, and there's less to lose. Lower-priced activities range from a night of back-slappin,' cigar-chompin' poker to more refined diversions such as Scotch tasting and hosting a roast. And activities like barbecues can adapt to whatever themes, rules, and levels of formality you want your party to follow.

BARBECUE

We're not talking about some casual get-together in your back-yard with a case of beers and a slab of meat, though that's a fine option too. Your barbecue can be as elaborate and sophisticated (or boorish) as you like. Here are some ways to make it a truly manly event:

1. Ask everyone to bring a hot sauce and host a contest to see who can down the hottest one (have antacids ready and available).

2. Mix it up: bring more than just chicken and burgers and hot dogs. Tell people to bring exotic meats, such as ostrich, buffalo, maybe even snake (consult *www.888eatgame.com*). Also ask the fellas to bring jalapeños, zucchini, peppers, mushrooms, onions, garlic, and oddball sauces.

3. Host your own "who can eat the most hot dogs" contest. This is dangerous, bad for the body, and stupid, but that's the appeal. Takeru Kobayashi of Japan holds the world record; he consumed fifty hot dogs in 12 minutes to win the 86th annual Nathan's Famous Fourth of July hot-dog-eating contest.

4. Combine the BBQ with a Scotch or beer tasting.

5. Make it a tailgate party and drive out to the stadium parking lot of the groom's local team—whether or not you plan to buy tickets. Park all the cars into a circle or semicircle to keep the festivities private.

tip: The big question is: gas or charcoal? If you already own a grill, this is a moot question. Just remember that neither imparts a better flavor onto meat necessarily. Gas is easier to use—but be sure to buy ceramic briquettes or flavor bars. These allow you to smoke your catch with wood chips, such as hickory or mesquite. On the other hand, charcoal feels more authentic and you have that 30-minute waiting period where you can down a few beers before anyone can begin to cook.

Make sure someone is bringing cups, plates, knives, forks, napkins, ice, chips, salad, a veggie for the vegetarian, mustard, ketchup, pickles, dessert, and water.

Approximate Cost per Person? About $10 to $20.

How Far in Advance Should You Plan? At least one day.

Number of Days for Event? One.

Photo or Video Ops? Groom with tongs, groom with giant plate of ribs, groom with sauce all over his face, groom with apron or groom wearing goofy chef hat.

Booze Policy? Beer, margaritas, whiskey—okay, anything you like.

BOWLING

It used to be that bowling was a working-class, middle-aged man's game. Today, in major cities at least, it is a kitschy cool diversion with infinite variations. New York's Bowlmor Lanes (212-255-8188/*www.bowlmor.com*) and New Orleans' Mid City Lanes (504-482-3133/*www.rockandbowl.com*) are two trendy bowling alleys that offer night bowling (in which the lanes are lit up like casinos) and live music. You can also join a bowling team, or try your hand at leftie bowling (not as challenging if you're already a leftie). No matter what you choose, there is always the fun of the ritual: the exchange of sneakers for cool shoes, the selection of a ball, and the system of keeping score (whether by hand or computer).

Sample Scenarios

In New York, there are two classic bowling experiences: Chelsea Piers (212-835-BOWL/*www.chelseapiersbowl.com*) is a modern sports haven in Manhattan that offers all kinds of activities. But it's the bowling that draws the biggest raves thanks to the forty-lane state-of-the-art equipment including automatic scoring and extreme bowling, in which players bowl after 8 P.M. surrounded by black lights, Day-Glo pins, loud music, and fog machines. Rates: $7.00 per person, per game; $4.50 equipment rental (per person).

For a far different experience, visit the aforementioned Bowlmor Lanes. Built in 1938, this is Manhattan's only surviving bowling alley from the "Golden Age of Bowling." Now it's a retro-cocktail magnet that attracts local NYU students and others who like to drink and bowl—and get served by waitresses in short skirts and boots. The people who run the place have also created quite a few original programs including "Nightstrike," a special Monday night bowling club featuring glow-in-the-dark bowling and a live DJ spinning the latest house and techno music ($20 per person for unlimited bowling and shoe rental). Alternatively, you can rent the VIP Room adjacent to the bowling lanes, which accommodates up to seventy-five people. The hourly rate Wednesday through Saturday is $190 for a lane, $2,650 for a half floor (fourteen lanes, bar, VIP Room, and separate entrance), $5,450 for a whole floor, and $10,850 for the whole damn joint. Bargain rates apply Sunday through Tuesday and before 5 P.M. There is a three-hour minimum required when booking an event. Normal fees are just $5.95 to $7.95 a game per person (bowling in New York is pricey), plus $4.00 shoe rental.

Baltimore has its own variation, known as Duckpin Bowling. The main differences, compared to regular bowling: the pins are shorter and more squat and the balls are smaller and without holes. Born sometime around 1900, the game has reached a handful of East Coast states, but it's most popular in South Baltimore, where a couple of dozen lanes still operate year-round. It's a blue-collar sport for the masses, typified by lane owners who allow patrons to haul in their own cooler of beer, and nobody will frown if you light up a few celebratory stogies.

To play, each team member is allowed up to three balls in each of the ten frames. As in traditional bowling, knocking all the pins down with one ball is a strike, using two balls is a spare. Unlike traditional bowling, a third ball is available, if necessary, to send all the ducks flying. Think it's easy? The pros—yes, there are professional duckpin bowlers—feel fortunate to roll a 170. And for those new to playing with these balls? You're lucky to roll a 100. White Oak Duckpin Lanes can be reached at 301-593-3000. Related games include ten-pin bowling and candle-pin bowling.

For more information on bowling at New Orleans' Mid-City lanes (aka Rock and Bowl) see the description of activities in the chapter "Hotspots" on New Orleans (page 217).

Approximate Cost per Person? In New York, it's $5.00 to $10 a game per person (about one hour), plus $4.00 for shoes. It may cost far less outside of major cities. Package deals are worth investigating; parties may rent one lane, multiple lanes, the whole floor, and/or private VIP Rooms, dance floors, etc. Expect to pay for mandatory catering at many places if you book a large party.

How Far in Advance Should You Plan? A few weeks to schedule enough lanes for your party. Ask about catering too.

Number of Days for Event? One day.

Photo or Video Ops? Great for action shots.

Booze Policy? There's a reason so many pro bowlers have a gut.

POKER BASICS

Cigars are a must. Beer is expected. Nothing fancy. Not only are there endless variations of poker, but everyone gets to be the dealer and the bets can range from the nickel-and-dime variety to a dollar and up. Still too pricey? Play poker with poker chips (or pennies) and arrange for the winner to get, say, a bottle of good Scotch ($40). That comes out to less than $5.00 per person. And you can play before or after other activities . . . with or without every bachelor party attendee.

Bachelor Party Poker Tips

It doesn't matter if you're a seasoned pro or a curious novice; you need to establish rules upfront and early. If you don't, then the stage is set for someone to feign misunderstanding just as he's losing a wad of cash. Next thing you know, the players start taking sides and the bickering starts . . . and nobody wants that.

Have everyone buy in at the start of the game; $20 to $100 is good.

Three types of chips should be doled out: pennies/nickels/dimes or $.25/$.50/$1.00.

Everyone antes value of lowest chip.

Dealer chooses game.

Dealer must explain rules if they are not clear to everyone.

You can raise only three times per round.

Maximum raise always equals value of highest chip.

No fewer than three at a table and no more than eight—get another table for big parties.

If dealer screws up in any way, it's a misdeal and he must shuffle and redeal—man to his right cuts the deck prior to dealing.

Invoke a freeze-out rule: Players must drop out of the game when they've lost all of their original buy-in. Losers may stay at the table, talk shit, and drink beers.

Quick Guide to Ranking of Hands from High to Low

Everyone forgets and/or fights over this, so copy it down or tear it out.

Five of a Kind (if you play with wild cards)
Royal Flush
Straight Flush
Four of a Kind
Full House
Flush
Straight
Three of a Kind
Two Pair
Pair
High Card

Sample Scenario

If you rent a suite at a high-quality, snazzy hotel (like the Windsor Court, Hilton Riverside, or Monteleone, for example, in New Orleans), you can eat, drink, and play poker while overlooking a great view of the mighty Mississippi River or perhaps the lights of the French Quarter sparkling below. Call the hotel and ask if they can supply a table, cards, and poker chips. Make sure the hotel room you rent doesn't have mirrors on the ceiling—seriously.

Approximate Cost per Person? Anywhere from $5.00 and up for the gambling. Add the costs of beer and cigars and you can still call it a night without spending more than $20.

How Far in Advance Should You Plan? Hell, you can call everyone that *day* and have 'em come to a hotel room or—cheaper still—host it at someone's apartment or house.

Number of Days for Event? One night.

Nine Poker Games

Draw

In most Draw poker games, each player is dealt five cards face down and can trade in up to three (always done at one time). Draw is the oldest form of poker and still one of the best. Since each player receives five cards before the draw, there is a limit to how many people can play the game. Here are some variations:

Jacks or Better

This is the standard game for Draw poker. The name of the game means that a player must have a pair of jacks or better in his first five cards in order to open the betting. If no one can muster it, there is an additional ante and a new deal.

Lowball

This game is dealt like ordinary Draw, but rewards the worst hand. Still, the winnings will almost always go to the best players. Superior gamblers will call the opening bet only if they have four non-paired low cards. In most modern poker circles, straights and flushes do not count as high hands, in which case the straight A-2-3-4-5, called a "wheel," is the best possible hand. In other circles, A-2-3-4-6 in different suits is the best hand. Make sure each player knows the house rules.

Stud

Five-Card Stud

Five-Card Stud is the classic big-money poker game, often seen in movies. The mechanics are simple: After the ante, each player receives a down card and an up card. A round of betting, calling, and perhaps raising ensues. Another up card is dealt to the active players, and another round of betting follows. And so on, until the last up card has been received. Final round of betting: showdown. No drawing of fresh cards is allowed. It's a tough, tight game and, if played properly, can become a bit boring when a reasonable limit is imposed on the betting. Most players want a little more action, so here are some variations to loosen up play.

New York Stud

Adding more hands to the hierarchy will generate more action at the table. In New York Stud, a four-card flush beats a pair, but loses to two pairs. A four-card straight will beat a pair, but loses to a four-card flush. Other special hands include a blaze—five face cards, which beats two pairs but loses to three of a kind.

Sudden Death

Think of Sudden Death as the Five-Card Stud version of Lowball, in which the sorriest hand brings home the pot. It's a risky game, as a face card or a pair can completely ruin a developing hand. Also note that a bet follows each up card, making it expensive to stay in. Smart players fold if they can't beat the up cards in each hand around the table.

High-Low Poker

In this form of poker, the high and low hands split the pot. This entices more people to stay in, and increases the size of the pots.

Seven-Card Stud High-Low

The Seven-Card Stud version of High-Low is one of the best modern poker games. The high and low hands split the pot, which makes for almost twice the action of regular seven-card stud.

In a seven-card game, five cards can be counted for low and five for high, with some cards going both ways. Thus, one player can make a good low hand and a good high hand, such as a flush. A seven-card hand like 2-3-5-6-7-8-9 can be declared 2-3-5-6-7 as low and 5-6-7-8-9 (a straight) as high.

Five-Card Stud High-Low

You're better off playing for high in this game, since a pair or a face card quickly renders a low hand not low enough. After the ante, each player receives a down card and an up card, and then bets. Each player who calls the bet receives another up card. And so on, until each active player has four up cards and one down card. Since each player has only five cards, the chances for winning both ways are slim; play for a high hand.

Widow Poker

In this form of poker, each player receives one or more down cards, with the number depending on the exact game (five-card or seven-card). In some games, each player can choose the hand from a total of ten cards—five down and five in the widow. The rest of the cards are turned up in the middle, and are common to all hands.

Spit in the Ocean

In this original form of Widow Poker, each player receives four down cards. An up card, common to all players, is dealt in the middle. It is wild, as are the other three similar cards in the deck. Each player discards and draws up to three cards before the final bet.

Texas Hold 'Em

This relatively new game is quite popular in casinos and high-stakes private games. Each player receives two down cards, followed by an opening round of betting. Three cards are turned up all at once in the middle for common use. Another round of betting ensues, before another card is dealt face up in the middle. Another bet, another up card, and then a final bet takes place. By this point, the pot should be hefty. Since each player receives only two down cards, Texas Hold 'Em works well for a large group.

Photo or Video Ops? Classic photo: Groom with cigar in mouth, surrounded by his buddies and booze. Even better if you can find a green felt table.

Booze Policy? Whatever you like. But beware: the more you drink, the more you'll lose.

SCOTCH TASTING

Few spirits have as macho and yet sophisticated a reputation as Scotch (which is a form of whiskey). Cowboys drank it, heroes drank it to numb their pain, and my dad drank it. At the same time, elite spirit connoisseurs dole out $100 or more for top-grade hooch, pontificating on its taste: sweet or smoky, dry or wet, smooth or harsh. Scotch is also a versatile drink that can be enjoyed straight up, on the rocks, or in mixed drinks. Diverse as Scotch and its drinkers may be, Scotch-tasting parties are a different story and follow far stricter rules.

Below are the tools, vocabulary, and process you'll need to compare and contrast Scotches.

What You Need
- At least three bottles of good Scotch—more is better
- A pitcher of water
- An empty pitcher for dumping unused Scotch in the wimpy event that someone doesn't drink all he's been given
- One tulip-shaped glass for Scotch and one lowball glass for water (per person)
- Some bland and dry finger food, such as plain crackers or toast (better than chips and pretzels, which may affect the taste buds)

Backgrounder #1: Single Malts vs. Blends

There are two kinds of Scotches: single malts and blends. If you remember nothing else, you should know the distinction.

Single malts come from one distillery. There may be many barrels used and many bottles produced, but this is like a pure strain. The best-selling single malts include Glenlivet, Glenfiddich, and the Macallan. I like smoky Scotches like Lagavulin and Laphroaig.

Blended Scotches are combinations of various single malts and grain whiskey—could be up to thirty or forty single malts in one blend. Popular blends include Chivas Regal, Dewar's, Johnnie Walker, and Cutty Sark.

Scotch snobs have historically preferred single malts, but there are plenty of good blends to be delicately sipped . . . or chugged.

Backgrounder #2: The Vocabulary

We've compiled some words commonly used to describe Scotch. Run these through your head as you are drinking and certain words will leap out at you. Drink a little more and you'll be lucky if you can remember any of them:

Peaty, smoky, vanilla, sweet, salty, oaky, fruity, silky, fresh, fragrant, spicy, minty, buttery, complex, grassy, bright, floral, lean, syrupy, dry, or "like crap."

Also see if you detect any of these flavors: pears, roses, violets, apples, bananas, cream soda, honey, lemonade, almonds, leather. Some people have said that the peaty Scotches taste like Band-Aids and sewer water, too.

Backgrounder #3: The Four Regions of Scotland

It's worth noting where your Scotch comes from since this directly affects the taste. Lowland Scotches are said to be dry and light, Highland Scotches are described as sweeter and richer, and Islay (pronounced EYE-lah) Scotches typically boast the smokiest flavor. But it's impossible to describe how all Scotches from a particular region taste since the ultimate flavor is also contingent upon the source of water, the barrels used for aging, and a host of other arcane, sometimes superstitious factors (such as the shape of the dents in the still). Our advice: If you're hosting a tasting, try to find Scotches from all four main regions:

- Highlands
- Lowlands
- Islay
- Speyside

The Process

1. Cleanse your palate by drinking a few sips of water.
2. Pour a shot—known in the whiskey circles as a "dram"—of one of the Scotches into each person's glass.
3. Hold the glass up to the light and observe the color—gold, yellow, amber, clear? If you want to call it piss-yellow, go ahead.
4. Ask everyone to note the aroma (see the vocabulary list above). Swirl it around, gently. Don't go on about the "legs." That's wine talk.
5. Now, finally, have everyone sip and note the flavors. How did it taste going down? Was there an aftertaste? Did it linger? Do you want more? Of course you do.
6. Add a splash of water. No, not carbonated. This brings out the aromas and flavors.
7. Repeat steps four and five, noting how the water brings out the flavors.
8. Have a cracker. You need something in your stomach.
9. Open another bottle and repeat steps one through eight.

10. Discuss findings: Does price make a difference? Can you distinguish an Islay from another region? Let's hope so.

11. Stop when you no longer care how your Scotch looks or smells or tastes.

Approximate Cost per Person? A typical bottle of Scotch costs $20 to $25; better bottles cost between $40 and $80. All you need is four or five bottles to have a proper tasting. More than six and your taste buds will likely be as drunk as you are.

How Far in Advance Should You Plan? This is another last-minute option since it requires only money for Scotch—and a table and glasses.

Number of Days for Event? Let's hope one day is all you need.

Photo or Video Ops? Add cigars and you have a real manly environment. Or just wait for the groom to get shit-faced.

Booze Policy? A redundant question.

ARCADE/AMUSEMENT PARK

Theme parks and arcades are not necessarily child's play. X-treme sports fans can prowl the parks for the scariest roller coasters and cruise for chicks. Car enthusiasts might prefer the idea of scouring the area for the best bumper cars and cruising for more beer. Go to a place like Coney Island in Brooklyn and you can stroll down the boardwalk and sunbathe on the beach, too.

Some of the Most Popular Amusement Park Destinations Are:

- Paramount Parks, like Great America (California, North Carolina, Ohio, Virginia)
- Six Flags Parks, like Great America, Magic Mountain (New York, California, Texas, Kentucky, Maryland, Colorado, Mis-

souri, Oklahoma, New Jersey, Washington, Illinois, Ohio, Los Angeles, Massachusetts)
- Knott's Berry Farm (California)
- Disneyland/World (Los Angeles, Florida)
- Rye Playland (New York)
- Coney Island (New York)
- Busch Gardens (Tampa Bay, Florida, and Williamsburg, Virginia)
- Universal Studios (California, Florida)

These places host corporate events all the time. They work with party planners, they hire their own party planners, they have places to chow down (like picnic areas), and they cater. This could be an easy way to foist the planning onto someone else. But these aren't the only options.

Arcades, too, have grown up since the boom in video gaming. Steven Spielberg opened up several Game Works (*www.game works.com*) facilities around the country, starting in 1997. They all offer restaurants, bars, and loads of games. A key attraction is Vertical Reality, the one-of-a-kind interactive video game combining a more than three-story-high screen with mechanical seats, simulating an actual twenty-four-foot, high-speed free fall. Game Works also features classic video games like Centipede, PacMan, and Asteroids. And if you like old-school analog games, you can always play pool, air hockey, or darts. Game Works has locations in Irvine, California; Ontario, California; Las Vegas, Nevada; Tempe/Phoenix, Arizona; Grapevine/Dallas, Texas; Seattle, Washington; Chicago/Schaumburg, Illinois; Detroit/Auburn Hills, Michigan; Columbus/Easton, Ohio; Miami, Florida; Sawgrass Mills/ Fort Lauderdale, Florida; and Tampa/Ybor City, Florida.

A similar chain is Dave & Buster's (*www.daveandbusters.com*), a seventy-thousand-square-foot arcade that offers billiard tables, shuffleboard, basketball hoops, virtual reality, a "turbo ride" motion-based simulation theater, and an Indoor Golf Simulator. Reservations are required for tee time. They now operate thirty-one locations across the United States, listed on an interactive map on the company's Web site.

New York has its own mini-mall-like entertainment center known as Chelsea Piers (212-336-6000/*www.chelseapiers.com*). For well under $100 per person, you could create your own decathlon: bowling ($6.25/game); ice skating (indoor and outdoor rinks, $11 fee plus $5.00 skate rental); batting cages (ten pitches for a buck); hoops on the b-ball court for just $7.00 an hour; replays of all your favorite *Caddyshack* scenes at the golf range ($15 for ninety-four balls); a ten-thousand-square-foot climbing wall ($17 per person)—not to mention weightlifting, soccer, swimming, and running. It's also got a few more jock opportunities, like kayaking and boxing, though they're also a bit more costly; an hour of boxing instruction will run roughly the same as two to three lap dances.

Approximate Cost per Person? Theme parks: figure $50 per person and up (this doesn't include food and beverages). Arcades: estimate $50 and up, per person, if you plan on having any fun.

How Far in Advance Should You Plan? One month if you have to reserve anything (space, food, etc.); otherwise, it can be last minute.

Number of Days for Event? One is plenty.

Photo or Video Ops? The usual groom-screaming-hands-over-head-in-the-roller-coaster shot. Or deeply concentrating on a game of Space Invaders.

Booze Policy? Most parks and arcades serve beer.

PUB CRAWL

Explore a neighborhood, flirt with the locals, and maybe make a game of it. Rather than blindly stumbling from bar to bar—which is a fine option too—you might come up with a bunch of rules first. Perhaps the groom does a shot of Tequila at every bar, before he drinks anything else. Or maybe he has to find a girl who'll let him drink the shot from her navel. I never had the guts/motivation to do this, but maybe if I were a harmless and sozzled soon-to-be-groom. . . .

Alternatively, you can agree on organizing a tournament. Make your last bar, perhaps, one that offers billiards or darts—or go to a billiards club, most of which serve alcohol anyway. Or take over a local sports bar and watch a game with the guys. Finally, you could cap the night with a karaoke bar, strip club, or cigar bar. Write down the name and location of each bar before you make the trek en masse.

Approximate Cost per Person? Plan on $25 to $50—remember you'll be contributing to the groom's bar bill too. Buy him the good stuff while you're at it.

How Far in Advance Should You Plan? At least a few minutes.

Number of Days for Event? One night.

Photo or Video Ops? Catch the groom cavorting with strange drunk girls or holding a pint at every bar.

Booze Policy? More more more.

HOST A ROAST

Not formal enough to be serious and not casual enough to seem hastily put together, roasts are a great way for a bunch of guys to show their love for the groom without seeming all misty-eyed about it. It's cheap, easy to organize, and cruelly fun. The one drawback: attendees need to come prepared.

Everyone presents a brief roast at some point, often after a dinner (best if you eat in a private area). Roasts may include (dirty) jokes, anecdotes, memories, exaggerations, and so on. Everyone also drinks throughout. And not all the jokes need to be mean-spirited jabs at Mr. Marrying Man. There should be some mean-spirited jokes directed at the other attendees too. Source material should be easy since these are the guys who have known the groom for a long time. Think back to camp, school, college, ex-girlfriends, old cars, old dreams, old promises. Now make fun of it all.

Each guy steps up to the podium (or front of the group) and waxes poetic. Don't wing it; come prepared with jokes. Don't go on too long; you really do want to leave 'em wanting more. Five minutes per person is plenty. Practice in front of a mirror—or live crowd—before attempting to do this on the night of the bachelor party. Remember: This can be a great start to a night but it need not be all you do. And if you want to have a surprise guest, here's the perfect opportunity to fly someone in from out of town—or have a stripper show up.

Ideal locations for such an event include private dining rooms and hotel rooms. Combine this with a steak dinner and a girl jumping out of a cake and you have an authentic, even classy, retro bachelor party.

Approximate Cost per Person? Figure on $20 and up, depending solely on booze consumption.

How Far in Advance Should You Plan? A few weeks. Give the guys time to rehearse their schtick.

Number of Days for Event? One day of roasting to sum up a lifetime.

Photo or Video Ops? Ideally, all the guys are dressed to the nines in suits or tuxes like a real celebrity roast.

Booze Policy? To suit the ambience, cocktails are better than beer.

DANCING/CLUBBING

Nightclubs offer an ambience somewhere in between a loud bar and a strip club. The music's blaring, the crowd may be packed in, the bar is ready to please, and most important, there are lots of lovely ladies. In fact, this is perhaps the best place to find cute, fit women wearing minimal outfits and shaking their booties *for free.*

The bachelor party can splinter off into groups, buy the groom shots, dare him to dance with super-hotties, or just admire the girls from afar. If you approach a group of women and explain the situation ("it's his bachelor party . . ."), they'll at least understand why you're drunk and hanging out with a pack of men. If they're kind, they may even treat Mr. Bachelor boy to a good time on the dance floor.

Remember to pay for the groom's cover fee (which could be $20 on a weekend night) and for his drinks. And consult your local hipster or any city guide to find out what's going on at the clubs *on the night you plan to attend.* Why? It could be world music night. Or S&M night. Or lesbians-only night. Wipe that grin off your face.

Sample Scenario

Billy Bob's Texas (817-624-7117/*www.billybobstexas.com*) in Fort Worth calls itself the "World's Largest Honkytonk." With 127,000 square feet of dancing, the bachelor party can just show up and it probably won't be the only one. Widely recognized as the best venue for country music performances, the club features

pro bull riding (now *there's* a photo op) every Friday and Saturday night, a huge dance floor, video games, forty bar stations and hundreds of big-haired North Dallas women. On one occasion, Merle Haggard bought drinks for the house. Tickets go for $5.50 and up (sometimes as high as $20), depending on the band. Reservations aren't required, but there's always the chance that a show will sell out. So unless you want your low-end bash to end up as a tailgate party, play it smart and make the call. Did I mention that the joint once sold 16,000 beer bottles at a Hank Williams, Jr., concert?

Approximate Cost per Person? Figure a $20 cover fee, $40 for drinks, plus 2 A.M. food runs.

How Far in Advance Should You Plan? Just call that week so you know what kind of music—and clientele—to expect. Consider arriving in intervals so you don't have twenty men trying to enter simultaneously.

Number of Days for Event? One.

Photo or Video Ops? Leave the camera home for this part of the evening.

Booze Policy? By all means.

KARAOKE

There's a whole world of karaoke out there—bars, players, software, microphones, mixers, CDs, and DVDs. It's big business. And fans are, well, fanatical. It makes sense since most people who sing along are drunk or on the way. And it gets the pulse racing, not just because you're screaming over music and crowd noises, but also because you're probably aware that what you're doing is thoroughly embarrassing.

Bars can host various scenarios. Some just have a stage and a machine. Some have private rooms you can rent—ideal for a bachelor party. Find out what's in store before you drag twenty drunk guys into a karaoke nightmare. It's not for everyone, but it can be added to a night of pub crawls or it can cap off an evening in a hotel suite with whoever's left standing (some systems hook up to the TV, for example, and some offer slide shows so the guests can see photos of the groom's formative years, as he sings off key).

Approximate Cost per Person?
1. Free downloaded software for your computer: $0.
2. Store-bought software: $5 to $20 on average.
3. Rental systems: $125 to $500 or more (you can even have these mailed to you, anywhere).
4. At a bar: can be free or there may be a cover charge.
5. Video of the groom drunk and singing "Whoops I Did It Again": Priceless.

How Far in Advance Should You Plan? Weeks. You'll either need to reserve a private room, buy or rent a system—or at least figure out where the party will transpire.

Number of Days for Event? One night of bad howling.

Photo or Video Ops? Video is best so you can hear how badly the groom is singing.

Booze Policy? More people sing if they're drunk, so please do imbibe.

SCAVENGER HUNT

We're not talking about Easter eggs and cute little prizes and secret notes tucked under the couch pillows. Bachelor party scavenger hunts give men a reason to do dumb, fun things in a competitive environment. Ideally, you divide the party into teams (two or three or four) and set them off on a journey to find weird, sexual, embarrassing objects—or to capture moments. Give each team a Polaroid camera and plenty of film and this will be the way they prove that members of their team really did do all the ridiculous things outlined below. The team to complete them all—or the most—in a set amount of time, wins.

Some suggested activities, of varying degrees of difficulty, include the following. They are often given a set of points from one to ten (ten is toughest) to build an incentive for partiers to complete the most challenging tasks:

1. Find a random girl at some bar and get her to drink a shot from your belly button.
2. Buy a giant blow-up doll (woman or sheep).
3. Convince a cop to place handcuffs on you.
4. Photograph a woman flashing you.
5. Capture a member of your team mooning a really big scary guy.
6. Make one of the guys sell enough condoms, sweets, and lighters to pay for a crate of beer.
7. Take a snapshot of one of the groom's ex-girlfriends.
8. Get ten strangers to jot down why single life sucks.

PG-Rated Do's and Don'ts

Do—Bring extra cash—for yourself and your groom (including plenty of $1.00 bills for tips).

Don't—Let anyone know you have this extra cash (at least until the end of the night when you can buy pizza for your sorry-ass, cash-strapped friends).

Do—Wear clothes knowing that they will get sticky, smoky, and sweaty.

Don't—Assume it's casual and wear sneakers.

Do—Tell everyone how much the night will cost in advance.

Don't—Wait until the end of the night to collect these fees.

Do—Try to work with the hotel so they don't throw you out.

Don't—Tell the hotel anything if you neglected to consult with them.

Do—Remember a few details from the night so you have enough ammo to tell your girlfriend/fiancée what happened.

Don't—Call your girlfriend. This is a boys' night out and she can wait until morning to hear from you.

THREE
R-Rated Activities

Some guys will jump straight to this chapter, where all the traditional bachelor party debauchery is explained in loving detail. To them, everything else seems wimpy by comparison. Fair enough.

First, I should explain that everything suggested in this section is far more common than the politically correct crowd would like to believe. It's also harmless fun. When I refer to "R-Rated Activities," I am suggesting that there is booze, nudity, and perhaps some gambling. Nothing that hasn't been done before—for centuries.

Generally speaking, you can arrange to have or do anything you like if you shell out enough money. A few common sayings will help you negotiate with limo drivers, hotel managers, strippers, strip clubs, escorts, and other people for hire. They are:

1. "Your mileage may vary" (YMMV)

Not every stripper/escort offers up the same amount of, er, flesh (or enthusiasm) to every party. This is sort of a *caveat emptor* (buyer beware) for anyone buying sex-related services. A related acronym, YMWV, stands for "your mileage *will* vary," which is probably more accurate.

2. "A little extra"

This is the polite way of hinting at more than a striptease or a platonic date. You might ask: "How much for a little extra?" or

"Can we negotiate a little extra?" or "Does she do extras?" An equivalent phrase would be "extracurricular activities."

3. "Don't ask, don't tell"

Limo drivers don't want to have to answer your question about whether or not you are allowed to do drugs in the back. Just keep it quiet. And the men who run the Vegas strip clubs want your money, not your scruples regarding what's legal and what's not. Go with the flow, baby.

Location: Hotel Room, Bar, or Strip Club?

The R-rated bachelor party is not so much the time to toast what was once a wild side, but rather society's halfway acceptable mode of allowing your immoral friends one last-ditch shot to get you plowed, shove a stripper in your face, and pray you don't pass out. To meet these ends, you need a destination far from home. Here are your choices.

HOTEL ROOM

The big question is: Are you booking one room for everyone to party in or several rooms for the guys to stay during a weekend trip? Either way, the assumption is that there's something going on that wouldn't fly in a more public place.

ONE-NIGHTERS

Maybe you've rented stag films, maybe you've arranged for the services of two, three, or six professional dancers/escorts, or maybe it's nude oil wrestling in the center of the bedroom. If the hotel is hip (or desperate) enough, these aforementioned services can be procured through a quick, off-the-record conference between the concierge and a few greenbacks. Otherwise, your best bet is a hotel with a lot of traffic—somewhere where no one will notice large groups of men traveling in packs.

It's better to be up-front about this than to get a call from the front desk (or cops) inquiring if you are having a party. The hotel may be getting complaints from other rooms—or worse—getting ready to throw you out since no more than ten people are allowed in a room at any given time. Plus, they're going to see packs of guys coming in and going to the same room. You're not hiding anything.

> tip: Try to plan various stages of activities throughout the evening—not just a dinner and then a strip bar—so guests may duck out early or enter in late. (See the chart at the end of this book for a mix-and-match activity list.)

If management says yes, it's still best to make all the arrangements yourself. You'll have to import your own alcohol, of course, because even the most robust mini-bar ain't gonna cut it. And you'll have to think about background noise—TV, movies, music, or conversational chatter? Complete control over the party environment has its benefits: no last call, you don't have to go home, and you can sleep off the hangover without stepping outside.

"*My place, your place, or here?*"

tip: Rather than renting a hotel room, consider a professional "party space." This might be a restaurant, club, mansion, or museum. You can rent furniture and have it dropped off and picked up. Chances are, you'll be allowed to do whatever you like, without worrying about noise, neighbors, secrecy, and the potential legal implications of your debauchery. Some spaces are free if you buy drinks from their bar or guarantee a big enough party.

MULTIPLE HOTEL ROOMS

Many bachelor parties now take place for a whole weekend or longer. The guys in this case share as many rooms as they need to accommodate everyone. Often this means two guys per room. You may well be lucky enough to get rooms next to one another, but not always. Inquire in advance.

Clearly, your party will be less conspicuous if you are not filling one room with twenty-five people for just one night. Therefore, you can easily arrange for anything you want without notifying hotel management. Still, you will want to remember to bring booze, props, music, videos, and so on. And don't forget to make one of the rooms a big space—like a suite—so the talent can do its thing without banging into walls.

BAR/NIGHTCLUB

Let's define our terms: When I say a bar or nightclub, I mean a partitioned-off wedge of some public spot, perhaps a local watering hole, favorite divey lounge, or semiprivate room at a karaoke club. If you can afford to rent out the whole joint, you don't have to worry about anything.

Of the three major venues in this article, the bar/nightclub is definitely the biggest pain in the ass. It has all the enforced decorum of the upscale strip club and then some, but no opportunity for reckless fun. You can forget about raunchy videos, ordered-in strippers, drunken bellowing, and just about anything else that might offend anyone (unless we're discussing a very divey establishment indeed). If you want your own music, you may have to import it, hardware and all. On top of that, many bars and nightspots won't be shy about requesting a fee for roping off some reserved, in-bar real estate. If a particular bar must be

> *bachelor saying:* There are "three rings" in marriage. There's the engagement ring, the wedding ring, and the suffer-ring.

included in the festivities for sentimental reasons, make it part of the "traveling bachelor party" and either arrive very early or don't go on a Friday/Saturday night. The crowds will soon swallow your party up.

THE STRIP CLUB EXPERIENCE

The immediate, obvious first choice for raw density of half-naked women per square foot (and the easiest ready-made "party" to whip up at the last minute, as though you'd actually put some planning into this venture), the strip club offers a made-to-order venue, a nice loud sound system, pricey watered-down booze, and possibly the best chance to embarrass the groom without actively ruining his life. Everybody knows that the bachelors get put up onstage in front of strangers to be toyed with and pho-

Tales of Whoa: #5

Her Name Was Pat . . .

I was with nine guys in a Lincoln Navigator, cruising to barhop. To make a long story short, five of us got blown by a pretty hot hooker. After she got out, and a block away, our Navigator was besieged by three fat hookers, who informed us that the previous hooker was a guy. Five guys laughed, the other five ran to a gas station on the corner to wash up. Looking back on it, it must have been the truth. The hooker in question was asked how much for the full monty, which she wouldn't do. She was then asked to do a striptease, which she also wouldn't do. And yes, I was one of the five laughing guys.

—Anonymous

tographed. It's so obvious a choice, however, that your party may be just one of a dozen others cavorting at the strip club you choose that night.

Even though the dancers (that's the polite word for strippers) see this kind of thing every day, too, they know how to stir up the mix with elaborate, staged pranks, such as pressuring the guy to do his own striptease (to the most god-awful music available, of course). What's he gonna do, back down like a wimp in front of the whole club? Most strip clubs don't charge large parties extra (sometimes there's a cover fee, sometimes there isn't) for the pleasure of providing a "space." The idea is that you guys are gonna be spenders, right? And there are enough females that every attendee can get in a lap dance or three.

But there is a downside too: There may be a cover fee of up to $30. There may be a drink minimum (two drinks) and these drinks might cost $15 a pop. The dancers may charge $20 or more per lap dance (plus tip). They may not indulge you

tip: You can start at a bar to warm up for the evening. Bars don't have cover fees, do have pretty women, and can accommodate groups if you arrive early enough.

in your every fantasy—for any price. And the club makes obscene amounts of money off the sludge they pass off as booze and they usually have very strict rules of conduct—no touching the women or getting too out of control. That said, you may negotiate to have some of the women perform a specific kind of dance to pre-arranged music if you work it all out in advance. For example, you could ask the club manager if he can get two of the dancers to pre-tend they are just visitors to the club and then slowly hit on and seduce the groom. Who knows what they'll charge, but it's worth getting creative.

Even though strippers make money by cleaning you out, you can do a few things to get more bang for your buck. Throw singles onto the stage instead of getting a lap dance; the money will last longer. Also, get the dancers to grab the bills from you; stick a rolled-up dollar behind your ear, between your teeth, or hanging out of your front or back pocket. Let her get it—maybe she'll get creative. It'll certainly break the monotony. Talk to the dancers. They will be flirting in the hopes of scoring a lap dance, but you can just milk the conversation for all of its sexual tension without shelling out a dime. Stop when she tells you she loves you.

How Do You Choose a Strip Club?

There are thousands of strip clubs (also known as men's clubs, gentlemen's clubs, adult clubs, and titty bars) throughout the

---

trivia: Attila the Hun was suspected of suffocating from a bloody nose after passing out from alcohol at his bachelor party.

U.S.A. Unless you already frequent the clubs in your area, you will have to do some research to find the best one for your party.

First, decide what kind of club you want. We're not talking about massage parlors or brothels (in this chapter at least). Instead, I am referring to the four major categories of strippers. From tame to wild, they are: bikini, tassles/pasties, topless, and all-nude. Usually, nude dancers work in places that don't serve alcohol. Some conservative lawmaker undoubtedly thought that Americans would have too much fun given that appealing combination. At some places, however, you can bring your own booze—though you may be charged a fee for doing so. Find out before you BYOB.

Another way to categorize strip clubs is by price and decor. Generally speaking, some are expensive ($30 cover) and some are inexpensive (free or under $10 cover). The more expensive, the more likely you will find a comfortable setting, upscale crowd, luxurious seating, and prettier women—as well as pricier drinks and an end-of-the-night bill that can total hundreds per person. These classy, higher-end joints are referred to as "gentlemen's clubs."

Far cheaper are titty bars, often sleazy places that you may find populated by locals and serving beer that costs less than $5.00. Here, the strippers dance onstage and cater to those who tip. Which means that a pocketful of dollar bills makes you a hero for the night.

If you have a chance, visit some clubs in advance to check out

Tales of Whoa: #6

First Come, Last Served

A group of college guys started a post–Spring Break tradition while they were still students—they'd go to McSorley's Alehouse in New York City, then hail a cab, hire a hooker, and get in line for a turn in the cab. The guy who started the tradition always made sure he was first in line. On the night of his bachelor party several years later, the group once again ended up at Mc-Sorely's, and they couldn't resist tradition—only this time, the rest of the group forced the groom to go last.

the vibe—and the clientele. At some, you'll find cute, young couples. At others, it's all mean-looking loners and drunks. You don't even have to pay to look inside; tell the manager or bouncer that you just need to set foot inside for a minute to scope out the place for a big party (better yet, call the club a day in advance and schedule a time to meet with the manager who will buy you a drink and explain the options to you).

Yet another way to gauge a club is to scrutinize the caliber of the women. In other words, are there women there that you (or the groom) find attractive? Some clubs are all white, some are all black, some are mixed. They may be cute or average. They may have enormous fake breasts or smallish natural ones. Tattoos or flawless skin. They may each have elaborate stage personas or just march out and get nekkid. The club may play dance music or heavy metal or both. These are details to consider or even request.

Finally, keep in mind that popular clubs are frequently crowded—so you might not even be able to casually walk into a trendy club on a Saturday night if you're bringing fifteen other men with you. So you can either call and inquire about making reservations at a nice place or choose a safer bet—like a dive—if you want to leave it open and play it by ear on the night of the party.

Where to Find Strip Clubs

The local weekly magazines usually have ads in the back few pages, and the Yellow Pages directory is a surprisingly reliable source for stripper and strip club listings. Strip club Web sites may be accurate but occasionally outdated. Nonetheless, some of these Web sites have gathered very useful information and organized it geographically so you can click on the city and state you are in to find out about the clubs, their addresses, their phone numbers, how much a private dance costs, whether they serve alcohol, how much cover charges are, and more. The sites are usually 100 percent free and updated regularly—as opposed to books. There is one drawback: 99 percent of these are just fronts for ads. I've gathered some sites on page 139 that seem to offer real guidance, advice, reviews, and credibility. But as with all Web sites, there's no telling if they will still exist by the time you read this.

Stripper Routines and Other Related Phrases

To be best prepared for that phone call discussion with the strip club manager, study the following common strip club dancer routines.

Bachelor Party Routines—If the strippers learn that there is a bachelor party, they will often call the groom onstage and publicly embarrass him. They may tie him up, whip him, tease him, give him a wedgie, cover him in whipped cream, beat his ass with a belt, put a dog collar on him, walk him around the stage like a dog, and/or humiliate him with whatever objects are at their disposal. One stripper was famous for sticking her heel into the groom's butt (well, not really, but it looked like it).

Bed/Couch Dance—The groom lies down on a couch or bedlike surface and the stripper dances, straddles, gyrates on and over him. This may or may not involve direct touching.

Chair/Table Dance—The groom sits in a chair and receives the same treatment as above.

Champagne Room—Legendary as it is, this is often just a private area that costs a lot of money. It may also be called the VIP Room or President's Club or Executive Lounge. The raciness of the act is to be negotiated by the girl, the groom, and his wallet. At Scores club in Manhattan, you pay $400 an hour to be with the dancer of your choice.

Feature Dancer—Most strippers start as regular house dancers and only hope to graduate to feature dancer. Feature entertainers are often porn actresses and models who tour the country visiting clubs and drawing big crowds. The club charges higher cover fees, but you may get to take a picture of the celeb or at least get her autograph.

Floor Show—This is any part of the show in which the stripper gets down on the floor and writhes, masturbates, dances, or looks vaguely gymnastic—often in mock orgasmic bliss and occasionally showing off her no-doubt-shaved crotch in the process.

House Dancer—One of the many strippers who regularly perform but have not yet graduated to be a feature dancer.

Lap Dance—Here, a stripper performs one-on-one with a customer, dancing between his legs, wiggling her butt in his face and rubbing her breasts and crotch against his knees and thighs. Men

> bachelor party quote: The bachelor party is a rau-
> cous, ritual demarcation between the chaos of single life and the
> mature orderliness of pairing off. One final night with the antiwife
> before wedding your wife-to-be, it's a time-honored way of saying
> "Good-bye to all of that."
>   —Lily Burana, ex-stripper and author of *Strip City*

are not allowed to touch the dancer at any point. There are several
variations on this including the air dance (aka table dance), where
the stripper gyrates but never touches you, and the friction dance
(no sitting on the gent's lap . . . standing dances only).

Pole Dance—Usually an elaborate dance that revolves, literally,
around a pole onstage. This is considered either advanced or silly
depending on your taste.

Private Dance—The groom is granted a private show in a private area on a song-by-song basis.

Shower Dance (aka Cage Dance)—The stripper essentially
dances nude in a stage shower booth; sometimes audience members are allowed to wash her down.

When to Go

This may seem like common sense, but many men forget that
strip clubs will be most packed on weekends. So if you want the
full crowd ambience, do go on a Friday or Saturday. But realize
that it's harder to get a big table or area for a group. Sundays
through Tuesdays are the slow nights and you will have easier access to both space and the dancers themselves. The groom will also
get more of the spotlight on one of these nights. Another little-
known fact: Some strippers wait until the end of the month to pay

> *tip:* To get the most out of a lap dance or table dance, don't touch the dancer (she'll retreat) and don't talk to her (you'll have some time to chat afterward).

bills. So you may see more strippers at the club in the last week of the month, compared to the first week.

Sample Scenario

At Scores, a major Manhattan topless club, bachelor parties have a few choices. They can eat dinner at the club (located in the front of the building away from the strippers) and then enjoy the dancers or cut straight to the stripping. They can also choose to pay a flat fee in advance for an open bar or keep drinks on a tab all night. Since drinks here cost $15 a pop, it's prudent to go with a flat-fee open bar.

A rate card (shown on page 137) outlines the options. The cover fee is normally $30 per person. Patrons can migrate to the Champagne Room (best seats in the house), but this requires either the purchase of a bottle of champagne or an additional $10 fee per person. An even more exclusive room, the President's Club, is available for big spenders and celebrities. Dennis Rodman has held several New York parties in the President's Club here.

Scores is not an inexpensive club, but then again, it is considered New York's finest—and the women are all knockouts. Most have tans and fake boobs. But there are natural bodies, too, and all kinds of hairdos, builds, and personalities. The club employs hundreds of women so it won't take more than a few minutes to find one or two that seem perfect. You won't find any skanks here, nor will you see obvious druggies or call girls. The club fires any

"Not me, lady—I'm just with the catering service."

women caught soliciting sex or doing drugs. Many of the dancers are college students so you can have real conversations with them. In fact, some rely on sugar-daddy regulars.

The layout is cozy and inviting. Step into the main room (maximum capacity is 468 people), and you'll see a bar at the left, couches and chairs throughout the room, and a small stage at the front. This is a gentleman's club environment (you can buy cigars and watch sports on televisions placed throughout the club). It is not a bare-bones strip club where men surround a long stage and throw dollars at dancers. There are no pole dances.

Instead, one woman may dance onstage, but a dozen others will be walking around the room at any given moment, working the crowd, each in a different type of outfit, offering table dances and sitting with the men who have paid for the privilege. Sometimes, two women will approach and ask if you want a two-girl show. You can decline at any time, though it's hard to say no when a gorgeous woman in a slinky outfit is batting her eyelashes and kindly trying to persuade you to let her remove her clothes in front of you.

If you see a woman you like, you can wait for her to come over or you can ask one of the wandering male managers to coax her your way. Once procured, she will remove her top slowly and gyrate around you (contact is not allowed, but it certainly happens). Her ass may hover by your face for minutes at a time, slowly grinding to the beat of the music, which is danceable and not too loud. Then you can buy another three minutes (approximately the length of a song) or watch her move on to another table. Occasionally, the DJ interjects with the introduction of a new dancer onstage: "Say hello to Britney!" She'll strut her stuff and then say hello to all the men plunked down in the chairs and couches around the room.

Since it is one of New York's major strip clubs, and located in

tip: Ask if you can bring your camera and/or other gear into the club. Some strip clubs do not allow bags or briefcases to be brought into the stage area because they have found hidden cameras snapping photographs of their dancers.

midtown, it attracts a lot of celebrities. Many male and female stars have dropped by to see what exactly goes on in here. The list, according to Club spokesman Lonnie Hanover, includes Barbara Walters, Russell Crowe, George Clooney, Bruce Willis, Jean Claude Van Damme, Mickey Rourke, Aerosmith, Motley Crew, *NSYNC, the Backstreet Boys, Heather Locklear, Pauley Shore, Mini-Me, Rod Stewart, Fred Durst (of Limp Bizkit), Steven Spielberg (!), Madonna, Mark McGrath (of Sugar Ray), and athletes like Yankee pitcher David Cone. Carson Daly and Howard Stern are known to frequent the place (separately).

A few stars have had their own bachelor parties at Scores, says Hanover. The late Chris Farley showed up at the Tom Arnold bachelor party (Adam Sandler and David Spade also attended) and was so inspired that he removed his shirt, got on stage, and strutted his stuff along with some of the dancers. Another time, Sandra Bernhard attended a bachelorette party here with some supermodels and joined the dancers onstage. Chuck Norris had *two* bachelor parties at the club—only one of which resulted in an eventual marriage (the other marriage was called off). Liam Gallagher, of Oasis, had a famously raucous bachelor party here too. Howard Stern's odd little friend Beetlejuice held his bachelor party here, but later announced on the show that the wedding was off. And Demi Moore reportedly conducted some research at Scores before starring in the movie *Striptease.*

At press time, another Scores club was under construction at Twenty-eighth Street between Tenth and Eleventh Avenues— which should be opened by the time you read this.

This is how the Scores Web site explains the various group rates:

Open Bar Packages with Food & Reserved Seating:

PLATINUM
$170.00 per person—Includes: 4 course dinner, admission & 3 hours open bar with tax and tip included.

GOLD
$145.00 per person—Includes: 4 course dinner, admission & 2 hours open bar with tax and tip included.

Open Bar Packages with Reserved Seating Excluding Food:

$130.00 per person—Includes: Admission & 3 hours open bar with tax and tip included.

$110.00 per person—Includes: Admission & 2 hours open bar with tax and tip included.

All Open Bars include—Top shelf premium brands, domestic and imported beers, house wine and house champagne.

tip: If you plan to go to a strip club *anywhere,* you must arrive early (9 P.M. or so) to snag enough seats for fifteen guys. After that, the clubs get too crowded.

Strip-Club Strippers vs. Private Dancers

At Strip Clubs . . .

Pros

- You can show up whenever you want because shows are ongoing
- There are a variety of strippers, body types, props
- Tipping is optional
- You've seen pictures of the women in advance on-line
- Written agreements confirm party reservations

Cons

- Grooms may not be center of attention
- You may get bad seats
- A designated driver or limo is needed
- Cover charges may apply
- Crowds are likely
- Drink prices are inflated
- There may be a dress code
- Local laws may prohibit alcohol if dancers are nude

Whereas Private Dancers . . .

Pros

- Undress where the beer is cheap and limos are unnecessary
- Ensure that the groom will be the center of attention
- Perform in hotel rooms or apartments
- Can get more risqué thanks to the privacy
- Dance all over the room—not a bad seat in the house
- Demand no dress code

Cons

- May not be as cute as you hoped and may not perform well
- Come to you—at a specified time only—and leave
- Expect tips
- May require partial fee up-front
- May not appeal to all tastes

Strip Club Review/Listings Web Sites

www.allstripclublinks.com   www.stripclubfinder.com
www.exoticnites.com   www.stripclublist.com
www.mensclubguide.com   www.stripclublisting.com
www.naughtynightlife.com   www.stripclubs.com
www.stripclubdirectory.com   www.tuscl.com

> *tip:* Ask hotel concierges or cabbies if they have passes to strip clubs. This may help you get in cheaper or even for free. But remember that cabbies may get kickbacks for sending you to certain clubs.

Strip Club Scams

Guys are at their most gullible when in the presence of seminaked, butt-wagging women. It's a phenomenon referred to as "thinking with the wrong head." And it gets men into all kinds of trouble—spousal problems, money problems, drinking problems. The worst-case scenario can trigger all of these. Yes, we're talking about stripper scams.

Sometimes it's a simple industry-standard swindle; drinks have always been watered down and overpriced. But other times it's more serious—as in outright theft. I talked to cabbies, club managers, and strippers to get the real dirt. Here's a look at the latest scams, with advice on how to avoid them.

DON'T TRUST THE CABBIE

In Las Vegas, strip clubs pay cabbies to deliver customers to their door—and not the competition's. The driver often gets whatever the cover charge is, per person. He waits until his new buddies (the naïve partiers) have entered the club. Then he goes to either the bouncer or a back-door manager and collects his fees. Clubs that don't play the game don't get any tourists. And cabbies will say anything to steer customers to a paying strip club. If customers ask for a specific club they've heard of (that doesn't require a cover fee), cabbies may lie and say the place is closed for renovations or out of business. So do a little homework before you paint the town.

Would You Like a Lap Dance or the Boot?

Lap dances at most clubs have gone from optional to virtually mandatory. Managers at upscale joints have to milk the customers for every penny they're worth to pay for the added expenses of comfy couches, prime real estate, and real DJs. If the patrons aren't buying enough lap dances—or drinks—they will be asked to leave. So don't go to a ritzy club if you're hoping to nurse one beer all night and ogle women from afar.

Bait and Switch

The women splashed throughout the local strip club's Web site sure looked cute. Too bad they're not the ones you'll see at the real club. If you're planning to host a party at the club based on the photos of the scrumptious girls on a flyer, print ad, or Web site, beware. Try visiting the club first or have them fax you some sort of photo verification. Same goes for hiring a stripper to come to your hotel room. The lesson here: Even if the woman moves on, her picture remains forever.

---

bachelor party quote: All men love to smack asses. I have no idea why.

—Former stripper

Tales of Whoa: #7

Maybe Marriage Is Okay

Sometimes humiliation is better than titillation. At one party, a rather overweight performer handcuffed the man of honor to a chair and dry-humped him until the chair broke. This wasn't the sort of erotic ecstasy the bachelor was expecting, but his friends loved it. So the stripper rode him some more, dressed him in some of her clothes, and covered his face with makeup. The result: no clinging to bachelorhood and no cravings for other women.

CASH ADVANCE OR CASH LOST?

Most strip clubs now have ATM machines. And, of course, there is a surcharge. But who's paying attention to a little added fee when a busty blonde is rubbing her chest against you? Open your eyes, and you'll notice that you might have spent $10 for the privilege of withdrawing your own money. It sure ain't gonna be $1.50, like at the corner store. So hide an extra twenty in your shoe and leave the bankcard at home.

HOW DID I SPEND $150?

You didn't. Some clubs tack fake purchases onto credit cards hoping that the patron either won't notice or will be too embarrassed to challenge the charge. If you were drunk, you may not even remember whether or not you ordered champagne, lap dances, food, etc. Bring cash only; it's safer.

SHIRT POCKETS AREN'T FOR CASH

As the dancers circle you, stare into your eyes, and pout those succulent lips, they are thinking about where you keep your money. If they see you taking $20 bills out of a shirt pocket or jacket pocket, it would be tempting indeed for them to reach in and grab the wad of cash. Especially if you're drunk. Keep money in a wallet and keep the wallet in a front pocket.

PRETTY MUGS AND UGLIER MUGGINGS

If you wave money around, bartenders, strippers, managers, and other customers will notice. It is not unheard of to be mugged in a bathroom or in a parking lot. Sometimes, the management may even be in on it—bouncers can make sure no one enters the bathroom until the job is done or they can prevent you from chasing after a thief. So bring a buddy to the potty next time. Have a fancy car? Better check on that too. Or buy a good alarm. (In 1999, two Russian women held up a guy in the parking lot at a club in New Jersey.)

DANCER DRINKS

"I'd establish my own drink, and it could be just orange juice," says Lily Burana, an ex-stripper who wrote a book about her experiences called *Strip City*. She wasn't allowed to solicit drinks, but the waitresses could ask men if they wanted to buy drinks for any of the strippers (as in "Would you like to buy the lady a drink?"). Guys rarely said no. Burana would then ask for "the usual"—also known as a "dancer drink." The guy thinks he's getting the stripper loosened up, but he's really just throwing his money away. At one Nebraska club, Burana had to sell six "dancer drinks" a night. This is common: Strippers often get a quota, and if they don't sell enough, then they may have to pay it off themselves.

THEY DIDN'T WANT A DRINK ANYWAY

In Vegas, many of the strippers can't refuse drinks even if they're teetotalers. Why? Because some club owners instruct their strippers to accept all offers since that's how they make most of their money. So don't try to come across as compassionate, kind, or rich; strippers are accepting your gifts regardless of whether they want a drink or not.

REALLY WEAK DRINKS

"I've been in places where they don't even tell you that the drinks you're ordering are nonalcoholic," says Burana. "Ask for a Seabreeze and you might get a cranberry juice with a lot of umbrellas in an opaque glass." Yes, fellas, you have been duped again. Might want to check on the ingredients before you order a Tequila Sunrise for her, too.

CASH AND DASH

You went to the local strip club and found a hottie to perform at your buddy's bachelor party. She asked for money in advance—a down payment or security fee. This could be the night of the party or weeks in advance. Either way, she never shows. Now you're screwed. The club's not responsible to cover her freelance work. And she may very well have moved on to the next city. What are

"Here's hoping you turn out to be a real crowd pleaser, Miss Howard."

you going to do, call the cops? Some women do this for a living—working just for a few days at a club before fleeing with cash in tow. A better idea: Go to an agency or independent stripper with a Web site or have the party at the strip club.

WHO ASKED FOR A LAP DANCE?

Some strippers have a nasty habit of dancing with a customer—unsolicited—and then charging for the experience. The stripper will start dancing near you and, after one song, she may say, "Did you like that?" You will say, "Very much" (would anyone say no?). Then she dances near you for five more songs and charges you $200. Next time, tell her, "That was great, as long as I'm not charged for it." Or complain to a manager.

DOES THAT INCLUDE TIP?

You bought two drinks, you're feeling good, and you decide it's lap dance time. You ask "How much?" and she flashes twenty fingers. When it's over, you peel off a twenty-dollar bill and send her off to the next patron. But she's not happy. 'Where's my tip?" she inquires. You have two choices at this point: Stiff her (and get no more booty that night) or grit your teeth and peel off another five. Next time ask if the fee includes tip.

The Entertainment: Strippers and Belly Dancers or Midgets and Fat Ladies?

You've decided to go with the classic bachelor party and hire female "talent"—strippers, belly dancers, girls jumping out of cakes, whatever. Enjoying this kind of show is as much about male bonding as watching the groom squirm as he realizes he may never again sample new flesh. Plus, who doesn't like seeing naked women? But questions remain: What kinds of women do you hire? How many? What do they do? How do you find them? And how much are they anyway?

STRIPPERS

As with strip clubs, the professional strippers come in four flavors: bikini dancers, tassle/pasty dancers, topless dancers, and all-nude dancers. If nothing else, make sure you know what you're getting before you book a night or pay a deposit. The most reliable source: a friend. Get a referral and you'll not only know what to expect, but the stripper (or her company) will know *you* are legit—and not a police officer out to bust someone.

Finding the right women for the right price won't happen with one call, either. Expect to spend several hours on the phone (and on-line) sorting out the details, looking at photos, even videos, and negotiating deals with various agencies around town. Don't forget that you guys are springing for a hotel room and libations too, which affects your stripper budget.

Exotic dancers and strippers charge anywhere from $150 an hour and up for the night, depending on whom you pick and what you want her to do. In New York, girl-girl shows, also know as lesbian shows, cost around $300 a dancer. Like the real world, you get what you pay for; beautiful women cost even more (and really homely ones might cost less if you can find a place that makes this a selling point). Consider booking two or three gals. There's a better chance that:

- At least one dancer will be pretty
- You won't get bored looking at one body
- The dancers won't get bored or scared of you
- You might get to see some interesting interactions

There are thousands of strippers in the U.S.A. and abroad. Some work at strip clubs, some work for stripper agencies, some work solo, some are prostitutes, and some are really just good at massaging bodies and egos. Like strip clubs, they place ads in local weekly magazines and post their own Web sites.

If she runs her own business, you will get a sense of what she looks like; she's not likely to fake a photo. That said, she can hide whatever it is she wants to hide. If you talk to her, find out if you can see more photos, via e-mail or fax. And go over exactly what she plans to do during her performance. Get it in writing if you can. Also ask if you may take photos during her performance.

Make sure the stripper (or her agency) knows exactly what you expect. One girl or two? Lap dances? Girl-girl action? Embarrass the groom? Some men think it's boring if the dancers don't do "extras," so make sure you know what kind of party—and dancers—you've booked. For information about coordinating raunchier scenarios for a bachelor party—including the possibility of sex acts—read the section on "Escorts."

tip: If you live in the town where the bachelor party will take place, go to a local strip club and find the most amazing dancer—one who you know will appeal to the groom. Ask her if she does bachelor parties. Then get her name and number (or business card). *Voilà,* your search is over.

For a complete description of common stripper routines, see page 130, "Stripper Routines and Other Related Phrases."

If you're dealing with an agency, beware of everything: price quoted, pictures posted, etc. You will have to work out a deal with someone on the phone and he or she won't care nearly as much as you do about who's showing up, what they look like, what they will do exactly, how long they will perform, how much it costs, etc. You can ask for a particular kind of dancer (black, white, Asian, busty, thin, nontattooed), type of show (lesbian, for example), costume (Britney Spears? Princess Leia?) and/or props. You can also explain what you expect the stripper to do to your groom. This can range from no-touching-him-at-all to a simple lap dance to a series of embarrassing stunts.

One thing that men seem to forget (or never learn): Strippers are not call girls. They are not obligated to have sex with anyone, for any price. While they all get propositioned, not all have a buying price. If you want/expect more than a sexy bump-and-grind, you better secure this from an agency that promises to deliver. Don't get mad at the dancer when she rebuffs your clumsy advances. Then again, it doesn't hurt to ask. . . .

tip: DO NOT assume that your stripper will have sex with anyone—including the groom. The right price can only buy some of the strippers, some of the time.

No matter what you want, phone manner is extremely important. It gets even more important with escorts (see the "Escorts and Brothels" section). Be polite and explain exactly what you plan on having, doing, etc. If you get the wrong vibe from the person on the other end, go with another company. It's your party and your money. And don't fall for agency bluffs, like: "If you don't book now, you may not get the girl you want." There are thousands of beautiful women who perform, so if you feel pressured, you can move right along to the next company.

Be careful that the other numbers listed are not just other lines at the same place—multiple stripper agencies are often owned by the same person. That said, some dancers work for multiple agencies because they get more business that way, so don't assume that the same photo on two different sites means that you have been deceived.

It's best if the company has a Web site, where you can see actual pictures/videos of the stripper roster and not have to visit an office or club during your lunch hour. If you're particularly thorough, however, do try to watch a video of the strippers performing their act at previous bachelor parties. Do *not* pay the full fee up-front for the stripper; the woman just might not show up. Instead, give a deposit—if necessary—to the agency/stripper and the rest upon delivery of the stripper you ordered. Deposit policies vary from state to state and company to company. I suggest you offer your credit card number, which appeases most agencies and protects you in the event of fraud. Other people have told me that they would never give out a credit card number. It really depends on the situation.

If possible, also get the name of the stripper and/or a description of the specific kind of stripper you want *in writing*. Bait and switch is extremely common; shady companies will send whomever they have that night regardless of promises made (remember that it's not really their fault if a nineteen-year-old stripper decides she'd rather go clubbing on your bachelor night). If the gal you wanted is unavailable suddenly, ask them to send a gal of equal merit; sometimes they will require you to pick an "alternate" too. This seems like a sensible thing to do since your first pick simply might not be available. It also means that they can't send a B-level performer when you asked for (and are paying for) an A-level performer. Some agencies will go over the stripper photos they have posted on their Web site with you on the phone. That helps. And some will contact other agencies to find a last-minute substitute. Make sure you get your money's worth.

Find out how long the act will last; chances are she has other parties to attend before and after yours. If you opt to stage the entire event in Las Vegas, the initial expense for you and your buddies may be higher—booking flights, hotel rooms—but there's no shortage of entertainment.

Even with all this preparation, you still could be fooled. Just make the best of the situation and don't forget to tip the dancer well—20 percent is kind. Keep in mind, most services will typically not send a dancer to parties with less than eight guests. And most strippers come with a body guard/driver. If you think they sent the wrong gal, don't let her in. Call the company and sort it out. You don't have to settle for someone you didn't want.

If you feel you have no choice but to admit the stripper who arrives, even though she is not what you asked for (she's short and dark when you asked for tall and blonde, let's say), consider stopping payment on the credit card after she leaves—which should only hurt the agency that duped you. But do pay the dancer for her services; she can't help being who she is and she'll probably dance her heart out for you.

If the idea of entertaining strippers in a hotel room bothers you, consider hiring a stripper to dress up as a waitress, bartender, host, or fellow pool player and instruct her to chastise the groom

bachelor party saying: If the bodyguard is a little guy, he has a gun. If he is a big guy, he doesn't need one.

tip: Offer the stripper and her bodyguard a beer. Treat them like invitees, not hired help. You may get more for your money—sometimes way more.

for being rowdy. Then, instruct her to begin to strip, mid-sentence, much to the (pleasant) surprise of the groom. You can make it a non-nude experience, often called a "strip-o-gram" but this is so tame, it hardly seems worth paying for. Nonetheless, it's one way to have a sexy stripper without betting the night on it—or offending anyone.

Stripper Review/Web Listings Sites

www.strippernet.net
www.stripperpower.com
www.101exoticdancers.com

STRIPPERS WHO JUMP OUT OF A CAKE

Nothing makes stripping seem as quaint as having the girl emerge from a cake. This is a time-honored tradition that only barely survives today. To most people, it seems like an old-fashioned, tame twist. It needn't be. Once the dancer has jumped out of the cake (usually not a real cake), she is free to perform whatever you have paid her to do. That can be a topless dance, a nude dance, or something more elaborate. Unless you arrange otherwise, the dancing lasts for one hour.

Here's a sample scenario: If you live anywhere between northern Illinois and Madison, Wisconsin, you can call up Wam Bam Entertainment (800-792-9822/*www.wambamentertainment.com*) and book a cake-jumping stripper for $300. Photos of the dancers are posted on their Web site. Choose the one you want and she'll

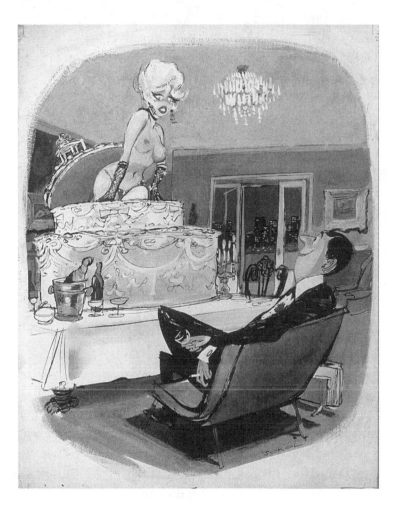

"I thought this was a banquet."

> *tip:* Strippers are usually late. They may be finishing a prior job, driving around looking for you, or just building your anticipation. Have a plan to entertain the troops for anywhere from thirty minutes to two hours.

arrive on the day you specify, rolling the faux cake (four feet high and four feet around) to your designated spot. While the cake is made of foam, it's decorated to look as if it's quasi-real with light-up candles. You then explain what cue will alert her to pop up out of the cake and begin her act. A driver, who brings the music and acts as DJ, will accompany her. It's very straightforward; just make sure that the stripping is done in private or that nudity is allowed in the public space you've selected. Pair this cake-jump with a roast and steak dinner and you have the perfect retro bachelor party.

STRIPPERS WHO DO "EXTRAS" (FULL SERVICE)

It's illegal for strippers to accept money in exchange for sexual acts. That's called prostitution. You're also setting yourself up for disappointment if you plan to ask the stripper you've booked to do anything but strip. That said, some strippers do indeed go the extra mile for a fee (ask if they offer "full service" parties). Few agencies will own up to advocating this, however (and neither will any strip club owner). Some might tell you that this is illegal and therefore they don't have women who do this kind of thing. Others may just say, "The girls are paid to do an hour show. What goes on after the show is not my business." As the saying goes, "Money talks." Did I mention that this is illegal?

Interview with a Party Stripper

QUESTION: What's the most annoying thing men do at bachelor parties?
ANSWER: They'll try to grab my crotch or stick their fingers in me. Repeatedly, even after I tell them not to. Or when they're drunk, they offer to pay anything to have sex with me.

QUESTION: How can the guys at a bachelor party make you comfortable?
ANSWER: I like a separate room to get ready, such as a bathroom. And I really like the attention when I walk in the door and the guys start screaming and cheering.

QUESTION: What does it take to get you to show or do more?
ANSWER: Money.

For more on women who offer "extras," read the section on "Escorts and Brothels."

BELLY DANCERS

Belly dancers, like strippers, come in all shapes and sizes—especially sizes. In some cultures, it is considered quite sexy to have a little stomach roll . . . it's womanly flesh after all. Find out how old the dancer is, what she'll wear, what music she'll be playing, and how long the dancing lasts. Does she bring the groom up onstage with her? Tell the person who's taking your order exactly

> *tip:* Remind the groom to wear clean underwear on the night of his party. The boxers may not leave his body, but they could well be exposed by an overeager stripper. Might as well share this concept with all the party attendees.

what you want. Do you expect nudity or not? If you want the party to be traditional and have the hooting and hollering without nudity, belly dancers are a good compromise. If the groom has a penchant for ethnic women, all the better.

MIDGETS AND FAT LADIES

Wacky bachelors deserve wacky entertainment. You have two choices: the midget or the fat lady. Each costs the same amount of money as a stripper. At Long Island Burlesque (212-967-7454/ *www.wildstrip.com*), you can choose among several odd characters, including Zula the fat lady in the African-styled getup; Samantha, the large lass in the leopard-skin dress; Bumpers, the big blonde in the red bikini; Tiny, who's not so tiny; Big Lou in the gorilla suit; and two dwarves named Scottie and Victor.

Escorts and Brothels

If you're feeling daring, most major cities have Yellow Pages, free weeklies, and Internet listings for a variety of escort services. While some companies really are just selling companionship with attractive ladies, most are selling sex with working gals (aka prostitutes, call girls, ladies of the evening). This is illegal everywhere except in a few counties in Nevada. So here's how it works in Nevada . . . but remember that some escorts will not do bachelor parties.

How Do You Choose an Escort?

The most reliable source is a friend who's used some woman or agency before. He can tell you exactly what to expect. Your next best option is to find someone who knows someone who can set this up. Referrals are always the best source. If you don't have any sleazy friends—or shall we say worldly aficionados—then you have no choice but to do your own homework on the Web and via phone. And the more research you do, the more likely you will find a woman who meets your needs.

Some Web sites, like the ones listed below, offer listings and reviews of escorts. They organize their findings by country, state, or city. They offer searches. They offer pull-down menus that let you specify all the characteristics you could want, like age, ethnicity, bust size, height, and weight—and sometimes much much more. Some escorts are now offering video ads, though these may be nothing more than grainy, twenty-second video streams. Still, it's better than nothing.

I'm never sure if the Web sites I find—whether purporting to be unbiased reviews or not—are written by anonymous strangers, members of some escort community, or the people who run the Web sites. So read reviews and testimonials with some degree of skepticism. Don't expect specifics up front, either. No escort service will come right out and say, "Sex for sale here!" Instead, look for euphemisms like ads that offer "full female companionship." This phrase also functions as a code when you are discussing what you want on the phone.

Some sites offer ongoing reviews from a community of Web

"She's truly a call girl's call girl."

surfers, and they seem to be legit. Again, I can't verify if the community is tainted with liars/scammers or not, but you'll feel safer at least reading the reviews at some of these sites. Two of the more prominent ones are *www.bigdoggie.net* and *www.theeroticreview.com* (which has a whole section dedicated to ripoffs at *www.theeroticreview.com/reviews/ripoffs.html*). Each offers reviews, but there's a membership fee to read the more "graphic" reports.

The Phone Call

You can't dial up and immediately ask, "How much for a blow job?" They will think you're either clueless, crass, or cops. You cannot *ever* refer to your true intentions, i.e., sex. If you do, your escort will likely leave immediately.

Instead, you play a little game. If it's a phone machine, leave your name (fake one is a good idea), number, time, and date of call (since the escorts and agencies may get hundreds), *and,* most important, general information about what you want (a bachelor party entertainer), including the where and when and for how long. Most people who call escorts are desperately looking to hook up *that night*. So some agencies and escorts won't even listen to messages that don't specify what day you are hoping to book.

When a voice answers, it may be an agency owner, a receptionist hired to screen calls, or an escort herself. Explain where you saw the ad and that you want to discuss doing business with them. You need to be generic in your phrasing at this early stage, but do mention that this is an inquiry concerning a bachelor party. She may be worried that you are some legal investigator. Or the proprietor may need to call you back. Either way, she'll use veiled language, never referring to "full-service" treatment (sex to completion) but rather stating: "Everything's negotiable." Wink wink.

She may refer you to her Web site or offer up an e-mail address for future communication; you'd be wise to create a new and anonymous e-mail address for this purpose. Don't ask her if she has a boyfriend or husband (it's none of your business), don't haggle over rates, and don't be offended if she asks *you* for a referral or some extra information about you. Do specify exactly what kind of escort you hope to meet. As with strippers, consider ethnicity, hair color, height, body type, costume, and so on. If you want to indulge in a kink of any sort, mention it now. Do not forget to mention that this is for a bachelor party; she may balk or charge more money. It's her decision.

Even if she's cool with the idea of a bachelor party, you still have to clarify exactly what you're hoping to see or get from these girls. You should establish as much as possible on the phone—before the dancers arrive at your door with their protective male guards. If you expect to see a live sex act with two women, say so, in as veiled language as you can so as to not sound like you're a cop busting prostitution rings. This may help you weed out the wimpy companies and find the gals who will "eat peach" as one agency once referred to cunnilingus.

Do not skimp. The less expensive escorts may well be more homely than you were prepared to stomach—and less likely to go the extra mile should the partiers get frisky.

Agencies

Agencies are tricky. On the one hand, they seem legit; each one has created an identity with Web site, photos, and phone number. Then again, they have been known to exercise some professionally misleading options, like not explaining all the fees fully, not sending the woman you asked for, and sending a scary guard to accompany the "talent." Independent contractors, as we'll call nonagency gals—do not incur the fees that agencies do—like the phone operator, the marketing—so they may give you more for

Escort Scams

There are seven major ways that escorts can potentially leave you wanting more:

1. They never show up.
2. They're really men.
3. The woman who shows up is not the woman (or type) you ordered.
4. It costs extra for sex; the fee was just a minimum (what was "extra" for a stripper may be "extra" for an escort, too, even though *you* thought that's all escorts did).
5. They perform halfheartedly and leave in a hurry (aka "dance and dash" or "cash and dash").
6. They act surprised when you make sexual advances, saying, "That's illegal!" and threatening to call the police.
7. They rob you.

your money. Read the reviews and use your judgment based on whatever phone manners you encounter. If she's rude or seems harried, let your fingers do the walking and go elsewhere.

How Much?

Expect to spend anywhere from $100 to $300 an hour for an average woman to as much as $20,000 per day for a famous porn star or model (they can cost thousands *per hour*). Some upscale agencies specialize in porn stars and models. No matter how cute or expensive, there will be different rates for out-calls (your place) vs. in-calls (her place). It's generally more expensive for out-calls since she has to factor in time getting to and from your place, gas money, and perhaps the extra cost of an accompanying guard. You may have to pay for the transportation—cab fare or gas money to and from your place—separately.

No matter where you go, there are always rules: no anal, no kissing, no fingers inside them, and so on. You will always wear a condom—sometimes two (this is known as "double-bagging" or "double-wrapping"). Technically, you are paying for her services as an escort—anything beyond that (including sex) is a matter of personal choice between two consenting adults and has nothing to do with money. Got it?

This is one reason why agencies may ask for an agency fee. You'll be paying the agency one fee for use of their honest-to-God escort (as in "companion") and a separate, and possibly large, "tip" to your escort when she arrives; the tip will be your way of thanking the woman (in advance) for her beyond-the-call-of-duty services. You can probably see how a scam could build from here. It's not unheard of for an escort to show up with scary thug at her side, ask for the money you agreed to by phone, and then explain to you that this fee only covers her showing up . . . anything else is extra and, by the way, prostitution is illegal. At that point, she may offer to hold up her end of the deal and dance for you for an hour—or she'll just leave with your money.

tip: Give good directions to any stripper or escort. They may get around a lot, but they also get lost a lot.

> *tip:* Ask the escort her name when she answers the phone. If she doesn't know (yes, it happens), this means she's using multiple names in ads to track which ads do best in which papers/sites . . . or she's earned a bad reputation with the old names because of fraud . . . or she's working for an agency that failed to explain that she needs to remember her stage name for this kind of phone call.

The Rituals

You will almost always pay for an escort's services when she arrives and not when she leaves. First, you discuss what exactly you'd like. Then she tells you how much the tip should be. Some people suggest that you place the tip—in cash—into an envelope and leave it on a table somewhere, as if to suggest that you are not giving her the money for sex (and therefore it's not really prostitution). In fact, there is nothing wrong with giving an escort money for a private dance, modeling, role-playing, or sensual massage. Still, the bag o' cash idea can't hurt. Then again, you may be able to pay with a credit card or even an on-line payment service like Paypal. These latter options are convenient and traceable, but you are leaving your digits with a stranger and the transaction might cross state lines and God only knows if that's a legal issue. No one said this would be easy.

No matter how you pay, she may have to call the agency to confirm that everything is A-okay. And she may ask you for ID. Show her a driver's license. She needs to know you can prove your identity. You now have her undivided attention for whatever time limit has been set. Yes, the clock is running. And she might make a call to her agency once again when you are done. Above and beyond all else: Treat her with respect and you (and your party) should be happy.

Escort Review Web Sites

www.bigdoggie.net
www.theeroticreview.com
www.adultbasex.com
www.eros-usa.com
www.escortamerica.com
www.escortplanet.net
www.escortplanet.net
www.fantacity.com/EscortCities/escorts.htm
www.outcall.net
www.thebestbabes.com
www.thefoxfiles.com

Model and Porn Star Escort Sites

www.exotica-2000.com
www.american-beauties.com

BROTHELS

Brothels deserve a whole book. They exist in all cities—legal or not—and everyone has an opinion about them. If you're serious about visiting one, you'll be wise to buy a guide or at least peruse a few Web sites (see page 167). It's worth noting that they are indeed illegal throughout all of the United States except for certain areas in Nevada (and neither in Vegas nor Reno). So all information in this section relates to Nevada brothels only.

Not all brothels are alike. There are small ones and big ones, elegant and down-to-earth, wham-bam-thank-you-ma'am, and please-stay-longer places. Here are some common questions that everyone seems to have but no one has really answered in any organized way:

How do you refer to women who work at brothels? "Working girls" is the preferred term. "Courtesan" has been bandied about, but this seems needlessly old-fashioned. Do not ever use the term whore, slut, or prostitute. You don't want to be called a john or a trick, do you?

How attractive are the women? Like the pool of real women in life, it ranges. Some are beautiful, some are not. Some are sexy, some are not. Some have fake breasts . . . all right already. You get the idea. Thanks to the Internet, you no longer have to wait until you arrive at a brothel to see the ladies. Many of them post photos of their gals. Nonetheless, not all the women work all the time so you must be prepared to accept a few possibilities. If there's one complaint, it's that some of the women don't look as young as they did in the photo. Well, that's expected. The Nevada Brothels Web site (*www.nvbrothels.com*) has an incredibly detailed summary of what to expect at each, along with pictures and many user-posted experiences.

How many working girls are available? Some brothels offer only a handful of ladies. Others keep a steady stream of up to forty women working at different times.

What's the minimum age of the women? It's either eighteen or twenty-one, depending on the county.

What's the minimum age of the men? Again, it's eighteen or twenty-one, though you can be sixteen if accompanied by a parent, believe it or not.

Do they accept women and/or couples? Some yes, some no, some maybe (depends on who's working that day). Most brothel owners are afraid that an angry girlfriend or wife will rush inside and find her cheatin' man in bed with another woman—and cause a ruckus. Increasingly, however, couples visit together, as they do to strip clubs.

Are condoms mandatory? Yes, by law. Doesn't common sense suggest you wear one too?

Is there a surcharge? Some places tack on an extra 5, 8, or 10 percent for credit card purchases. Others charge an additional $5.00 or $10 for every $100 spent no matter what mode of payment. Some have no surcharges at all.

Do cabbies get a cut? In some cases, the brothel may have worked out a deal to give cabbies 20 to 30 percent of the total bill. This is an incentive for cabbies, but it may tack on an extra fee for you and/or the working girl.

What's the minimum? There is almost always a $60 to $100 minimum. Straight sex usually costs between $100 and $500. Anything more costs more—and that includes massage, cuddling, and creative sexual positions. The rates go even higher for prettier/ younger women . . . and chumps. There is no maximum, of course. Some women, especially hotties, will not accept the minimum. This is one of those YMMV (your mileage may vary) situations. Most women split the fee fifty-fifty with the brothel.

Is there any racial bias? Sometimes, maybe. Black men, sadly, may get the shaft (so to speak) when it comes to escorts. Black men may be asked to pay higher prices for the exact same services that other men get, and/or they may not even get the full range of available women at a brothel—since some of these gals prefer not to work with black men.

Brothel Review Web Sites

As with strip clubs and strippers and escorts, there are many Web sites that review brothels, and in the process, offer necessary info like phone numbers, addresses, maps, pictures, descriptions of the experience, and a vague sense of the quality and quantity of pretty ladies. The ones listed here are 100 percent free and updated regularly.

www.nvbrothels.com
www.worldseguide.org

Brothel Glossary

Most brothels offer a menu of sexual activities from which to choose. You'll feel more confident—and be better equipped to haggle—if you know what the hell they're talking about. You'll also be better equipped to read on-line reviews, which frequently invoke arcane acronyms and insider phrases. Below are only some of the more common sex-related terms I've seen on menus and in reviews. I've excluded anything that seemed obvious (like "two-girl party").

Bag (also: Beret, Glove, Party Hat, and Jimmy Hat)— Condom.

Bareback Blow Job (BBBJ)—Oral sex without a condom (also known as "French Without").

BBW—Big beautiful woman, as in chubby or Rubenesque.

Blue Pill—Viagra.

Body French—The woman kisses, licks, and caresses the man's neck, shoulders, nipples, and stomach.

Cowgirl—When a woman is on top. ("Reverse cowgirl" is when she faces your feet and not your face.)

DATY (aka "Dining at the Y" and "Love at the Y")— Cunnilingus.

Full French—Oral sex to completion.

Full Service—Vaginal sex to completion.

GFE (Girlfriend Experience)—When a woman takes the time and energy to treat a man with consideration, affection, and interest, this is referred to as a "girlfriend experience." Often means she indulges the man in French kissing, cuddling, and/or massage.

Greek—Anal sex.

Half-Half or Half-and-Half (H&H)—Oral and straight sex.

Hobbyist (or John or Trick)—A man who frequents brothels or uses prostitutes.

Hot and Cold French—The woman performs oral sex holding liquids of different temperature in her mouth.

In-Call—You go to her place.

Lineup—When the women come out and meet and greet the potential client(s).

Madame—The female proprietor of a brothel.

Missionary—Man on top.

Out-Call She comes to your place.

Party—Sex acts at a brothel. As in "What kind of party do you want?"

Russian—When a man places his penis between a girl's breasts to completion (yes, "titty fucking").

Salt and Pepper Party or Chocolate and Vanilla—A party with one black lady and one white lady.

Viagra Party—Yes, you have to bring your own.

YMMV—Your mileage may vary. In other words, there's no telling how good or bad the experience will be. Also means: Don't assume that an escort/stripper will be as good as it sounded in that review you read.

$$$—This may mean the experience is expensive. More specifically, it can refer to monetary increments, as in $ = 100, $$ = $200, and $$$ = $300.

Sample Scenario #1

(**Based on solid reporting, but alas, not personal experience**)

You drive to the brothel. Park. Knock or ring the bell. Someone will size you up before opening the door to make sure you are not a freak, drunk beyond repair, or a crazed, vengeful wife. You will be asked if you are there to see the girls—or just gathering souvenirs (like ashtrays). When you explain that you're there for the real deal, the host (often a woman) will call in the ladies and they will introduce themselves to you dressed in some sexy ensemble, perhaps a robe or a dress or lingerie. This procedure is called a lineup.

On some occasions, you can talk to them in a large public room or in a bar area to get a sense of their personalities. Other times, you may be expected to choose from the lineup immediately. Try to remember their names or at least the one you would like. It is polite to wait until all the women have introduced themselves, and then mention that they are all quite beautiful and finally announce your decision. You may also take some time to think about it at the bar and watch the women line up for another customer before making your decision. But the one you want might walk away with another man, so it's a gamble. A bartender may be present—he may also be the security guard.

Once a coupling has been established, your new friend will lead to you a room and ask you what you want and possibly show you a menu of options. Common requests include straight sex, oral sex, or both. The quoted prices, whether she says them or displays them, will be more than she really expects. Find out what you are allowed to ask for and haggle a bit. Generally, there's no mouth kissing, no anal, no fingering, and sometimes no breast fondling. The minimum is around $100 for God-knows-how-little; you should expect to pay closer to $300 to $500 for actual intercourse.

"Half-and-half" is most common; this means you get a blow job and intercourse to completion. You pay extra for anything unusual, including snuggling, massages, and, potentially, sleeping the night with her. Again, the prettier and younger the woman, the more she can charge—$1,000 is not out of the question. Tipping is not required but often deserved (15 to 20 percent). Beware: Management may well be listening via intercoms planted in the room, and they may want 50 percent of the tip too. So don't discuss the tip aloud if possible.

Before anything actually happens, your new friend will ask you to shower or she will help you bathe. Afterward, she will roll a condom onto your now-turgid member. From here on, you're on your own. Once you're done, you're done. Could be thirty minutes, could be longer. There is no money-back guarantee for anything. If you cannot perform, you are out of luck.

Sample Scenario #2: The Bunny Ranch

When owner Dennis Hof acquired the brothel, he decided to make it unlike any other place he had ever seen or heard about. He wanted to make it warm and welcoming, with options found nowhere else. Some say he's succeeded.

"This is where all the celebrities and athletes come," says the publicity-happy Hof before rattling off a laundry list of stars who swear by (or work at) the place. "We just did Vince Neil's birthday

trivia: For about five years, the owner of the Bunny Ranch referred to it as a bordello and brothel, but too many people didn't understand what that meant. It's now called the Moonlite Bunny Ranch Cathouse.

> tip: Remember that working girls can be ugly, mean, bored, old, saggy, tardy, filthy, druggy, more expensive than you thought, and quite possibly male. On the other hand, they are wondering these things about you too. Plan for the best and make sure you bathe, brush your teeth, and dress nicely before the encounter—and act gentlemanly throughout. If you're careful (and lucky), she'll be young, hot, eager to please, and grant you more than you paid for.

party. Jesse Ventura brags about coming to the Bunny Ranch, and how all the girls look like *Playboy* Playmates. He wrote that in his book. And now we have *Playboy* Playmates. We have Teri Weigel. We have Sunset Thomas. She's been a *Penthouse* Pet four times and a huge porn star. We've had over a hundred and eighty XXX stars. And we always have a few in-house. As Howard Stern would say, 'It's the only place in the world where you can have legal sex with real *Playboy* Playmates, *Penthouse* Pets, *Hustler* Honeys, or XXX stars.' "

The Bunny Ranch is indeed different. According to Mr. Hof, there is no minimum charge. The gals choose who they party with and how much to charge. Women and couples are allowed to enter—not true at other brothels. Guys do not pick women out of a lineup. The Ranch won't force you to party with anyone, ever. And you can sit back and drink all day if you want. "Our place is the future of prostitution in America," says Hof.

Bachelor parties typically go off one by one with gals or have sex with the same woman over the course of the night—the latter option is inexplicably popular, according to Hof. "[They] usually want a two-girl show . . . and then they go from there deciding

Some Legal Brothels
(last I checked)

Most establishments are open twenty-four hours a day, seven days a week—and they take credit cards. Scams seem less pervasive here than at strip clubs, if only because the exchange of money for sex is a lot clearer than the exchange of money for whatever it is you hope to get in the Champagne Room.

Reno Area

Old Bridge Ranch
775-342-0223
4756 Peri Ranch Road, Sparks, NV 89434

Carson City Area

Kit Kat Ranch
775-246-9975
50 Kit Kat Drive, Mound House, NV 89706

Miss Kitty's Pussycat Lounge
888-MS-KITTY
95 Kit Kat Drive, Mound House, NV 89706

Moonlite Bunny Ranch
888-BUN-NYRA
30 Moonlight Road, Mound House, NV 89706

Sagebrush Ranch
888-852-8144
51 Kit Kat Road, Mound House, NV 89706

Fallon Area
Salt Wells Ranch
775-423-3005
12500 Austin Highway 50, Fallon, NV 89406

Winnemucca Area
Cozy Corner
775-623-9959
50 Riverside Street, Winnemucca, NV 89445

The Pussycat Saloon
775-623-9939
35 Riverside Street, Winnemucca, NV 89445

The Villa Joy
775-623-9903
30 Riverside Street, Winnemucca, NV 89445

Battle Mountain Area
Donna's Battle Mountain Ranch
775-635-2764
395 North Second Street, Battle Mountain, NV 89820

Elko Area
Chardon's Club
775-738-9923
357 Douglas Street, Elko, NV 89801

Inez's
775-753-5398
232 South Third Street, Elko, NV 89801

Mona's Ranch
775-777-7469
103 South Third Street, Elko, NV 89801

Sharon's Brothel & Bar
775-754-6427
501 State Highway 278, Carlin, NV 89822

Sue's Fantasy Club
775-777-8490
173 South Third Street, Elko, NV 89801

Wells Area

Bella's Hacienda Ranch
775-752-9914
619 Eighth Street, Wells, NV 89835

Donna's Ranch
775-752-9959
679 Eighth Street, Wells, NV 89835

Ely Area

Stardust Ranch
775-289-4569
190 High Street, Ely, NV 89301

Las Vegas Area

Cherry Patch/Mabel's Ranch
775-372-5574
Appaloosa Lane, Crystal, NV 89020

Chicken Ranch
775-727-5721
10511 Homestead Road, Pahrump, NV 89041

Sheri's Ranch
775-727-5916
10551 Homestead Road, Pahrump, NV 89041

Beatty/Tonopah Area

Angel's Ladies Ranch
775-553-9986
2.1 miles north on US 95, Beatty, NV 89003

Cherry Patch Ranch 2
775-372-5551
Highway 95, Armargoosa Valley, NV 89020

Shady Lady Ranch
775-553-9100
Highway 95, Nye County, NV 89003

who teams up with whom afterward," Hof explains. "On a typical Monday through Thursday, we'll have two to three and on weekends it's a couple a night. Could be four or five bachelor parties on any given night. We have two hundred and fifty girls working for us. It takes that many to keep forty working for us at all times, 24/7/365."

The Bunny Ranch also boasts deluxe treatment packages for bachelor parties—prices range from a few hundred dollars a person to thousands. While these options don't appear on any menu, the manager can take all your information over the phone and arrange to have limos pick you up at the airport (Carson City or Reno, which is thirty minutes away) if you like, get you cheap rates at local places (three-, four- or five-star hotels), provide balloons with your name on them (!), and procure other souvenirs (T-shirts, poker chips, sex menus). If there are enough people, they can even block off a whole section of the brothel. "When we host a party like that, only thirty percent of the guys usually have sex," says Hof. "The rest just want to have fun."

Videos

Movies are not only the cheapest way to go, they help you avoid the awkward moments and inevitable disappointments that come with other schemes. The most pressure you will have to face is

Tales of Whoa #8:

Don't Tell Mom

The owner of the Bunny Ranch shared this (supposedly true) story: A customer walked in and waited for the introduction to the women. When he saw his daughter in the lineup, he said, "What the hell are you doing here?" His daughter said, "What are *you* doing here?" They both started laughing, hugged, and right in front of everyone agreed: "If you don't tell Mom, I won't tell Mom."

picking the right set of films (you can rent ten videos for $30 and have enough content and variety to last the whole evening).

You can never go wrong with big names (Vivid Video, Seymour Butts) or outright absurdity (*Edward Penishands, Lactating Biker Chicks, Midget Madness,* etc.). If all else fails, refer to *Adult Video News* magazine or Web site (*www.avn.com*) for definitive reviews of titles such as *Nubian Nurse Orgy* and *Good Will Humping.* Videos make great mood-setters in the event that you also want talent/strippers to arrive later—and they almost always do arrive late. Just make sure your hotel has a TV, VCR/DVD, remote control, and thick walls.

CLASSIC VIDEOS

Combine the phrase "bachelor party" and "videos" and most people think porn. That's shallow and insensitive. Participants of male-bonding extravaganzas can enjoy many other styles of dirty, salacious, cheesy, and oddball films.

For example: You can host a swinging evening of cocktails with films of retro go-go dancers shaking their booties in the background. Alternatively, you can rent compendiums of NFL highlights or monster truck rallies or even manly war sagas like *The Dirty Dozen.* Or add a two-hour break in the festivities by screening some "classic" bachelor films (see list).

For racier stuff, consider classic old pornos and weird old movies that date back fifty or more years. It makes far more sense to amuse and/or disgust your friends than to arouse them—why get twenty men horny in a hotel room? Consider a quick visit to the local porn section of your video store, with the express purpose of finding the most awful-sounding title(s). Fetish films are freaky fun. *Enema Nurses, Fat Fucks,* or *Lactamania,* anyone? In many cases, the title or theme alone can make or break the viewing experience. But be prepared for grotesqueries the likes of which you never imagined.

To make the night even more interactive, the best man can develop and explain drinking games that correspond to the action and dialogue of the film. For example, when watching *Animal House,* you might establish the rule that everyone drinks whenever John Belushi enters the picture. Use your imagination and refrain from reenacting the "What Am I?" skit that Belushi showcased in the movie (answer: a zit).

TOP 10 FUNNIEST PORN TITLES ADAPTED FROM MAINSTREAM MOVIES

1. *On Golden Blond*
2. *Shaving Ryan's Privates*
3. *Intercourse with the Vampire*
4. *Pulp Friction*
5. *The Sperminator*
6. *Beatlejism*
7. *Free My Willy*
8. *Thelma Does Louise*
9. *Fleshdance*
10. *White Men Can Hump*

> *tip:* No matter what you watch, consider renting a giant
> TV/screen and DVD player—with remote, of course—since you'll
> want to pause (and maybe fast forward) at times, too.

TOP 10 PORN CLASSICS

1. *Behind the Green Door*
2. *The Devil in Miss Jones*
3. *Deep Throat*
4. *Debbie Does Dallas*
5. *Taboo*
6. *Talk Dirty to Me*
7. *The Opening of Misty Beethoven*
8. *Sex Boat*
9. *High School Memories*
10. *Insatiable*

RUSS MEYER FILMS

While celebrity skin seems to be the most popular screen con-
tent for bachelor parties these days, we'll pass on all the Pamela
Lee bootlegs. Instead, go for some real gusto and some gen-u-ine
wacko Americana: the works of Russ Meyer. He is not just a
"breast man." He is the #1 connoisseur of beautiful, overflowing,
oversized chests—and he's been that way long before silicone entered the picture. He has found some of the most astoundingly
Amazonian starlets ever filmed—hot-wired, hell-bent freaks of nature whose libidos consume the dimwitted men who drool over

trivia: The Internet Movie Database (*www.imdb.com*) lists more than ninety films with the word "bachelor" in the title, including such perennial classics as *A Crusty Old Bachelor* (1899), *The Last Bachelor* (1996), and *El Reprimido* aka *The Repressed Man* aka *Timid Bachelor* (1974).

them. And he's created an ample library of films to showcase the ample bosoms he so adores.

What's great about these movies, without getting too grad student about them, is their celebration of crude American archetypes and their deeply coded, modern adaptations of Greek tragedy and Jacobean revenge drama. And babes. Amazing babes! Babes like they don't make 'em anymore: Meyer stalwarts like Edy Williams (his wife for a while) and Uschi Digard are now old enough to be your mom (or grandmom), but don't let those Oedipal stumbling blocks get in the way. Check out *Faster Pussycat, Kill! Kill!* (1965), *Common Law Cabin* (1967), *Mudhoney* (1965) or, for pure, um, conceptual focus, *Mondo Topless* (1966). Meyer's most watchable, most plot-driven film is *Beyond the Valley of the Dolls* (1970), cowritten by film critic Roger Ebert. This is the kind of good, old-fashioned, all-American smut that never gets overly gynecological. Watch with pride.

Classic Bachelor Party Films

Just as there are two types of bachelor parties (PG- and R-rated), so too are there two types of bachelor party films. The first caters to the wild and wanton crowd; think pornos and any flick that's more flesh than flash (*Showgirls, Playboy* videos). Alter-

Tales of Whoa: #9

Battle with the Boobs

In 1998 a Florida man, Paul Shimkonis, made national news when he sued a topless dancer named Tawny Peaks for injuring him during his bachelor party. The injury, he said, occurred when the size 60-HH dancer whacked him upside the head with her breasts. "I saw stars," Shimkonis said at the time. "It was like two cement blocks hit me." Claiming bodily injury, disability, pain and suffering, disfigurement, and mental anguish, Shimkonis took his case to "The People's Court." He lost.

natively, there are those videos that make for good-natured, imp-ish entertainment after, say, a day of mountain climbing; think black comedies, bachelor party sagas, and male-bonding dramas (*Very Bad Things, Diner*).

20 Dates

Writer/Director Myles Berkowitz, a divorced L.A. man, goes on twenty dates in search of true love—and in front of the camera.

American Pie

Four high school students decide they must lose their virginity before the senior prom. Despite gratuitous sex and bathroom humor, this movie also has a heart—and a plot. Ms. Elizabeth is stunning as the foreign exchange student.

Animal House

Teen movies today just don't come close to this 1978 classic. It is John Belushi's tour de force and the source of many a famous quote. Here's some trivia for you: Martha Smith, who played Babs, was *Playboy* magazine's July 1973 Playmate of the Month.

Bachelor Party

Tom Hanks would cringe if he saw this today, but back in 1984, he was really just the *Bosom Buddies* guy. Here, he's a charming goofball about to marry an upper-class girlfriend, whose parents disapprove of him. His friends decide to throw a wild and crazy bachelor party . . . cocaine-snorting mule included.

Diner

Male bonding à la Baltimore circa 1959—with Mickey Rourke, Steve Guttenberg, Daniel Stern, Ellen Barkin, Timothy Daly, Kevin Bacon, and Paul Reiser. Could your girlfriend pass the football trivia test?

The Knack . . . and How to Get It

Though not well known, this British sex farce speaks to the bachelor mindset. Here, a timid schoolteacher learns how to make it with the ladies from his housemate. Look for Jacqueline Bisset in a bit-part—among many other mod, mini-skirted, Pill-liberated gals.

Playboy Videos

Search *www.playboystore.com* by fetish keyword: cheerleaders, sorority girls, wrestlers, biker babes, Spring Break flashers, and of course, Playmates. There's something for everyone.

Porky's and its sequels

The sophomoric yucks may or may not amuse you as much
twenty or so years after it came out. Still, it's a classic
bachelor party video with visits to the girls' locker room
and the local whorehouse. *Porky's* Trivia: This comedy also
stars Kim Cattrall of *Sex and the City* fame.

Sherman's March

A guy travels through the South, initially on a historical
quest, but ultimately in search of women. He meets plenty
of gals, but the highlights are filmmaker Ross McElwee's
insights at three in the morning.

Striptease

The only reason to see this is to admire Demi Moore's post-
boob job hard body. Burt Reynolds and porn superstar
Pandora Peaks make for fun diversions.

Swingers

Women can't believe men really think like this. Of course we
do. Jon Favreau plays the timid, bumbling sensitive guy
(who just broke up with his girlfriend) to Vince Vaughn's
slick Don Juan. Most of us are somewhere in between. No
other film so captures the modern (albeit Los Angeles–
based) boys' nights out.

Showgirls

Critics panned this flesh-athon when it first came out, but
now it's a cult favorite thanks to the catty dialogue and
eye-pleasing cast, including Elizabeth Berkley and Gina
Gershon.

Vampyros Lesbos

Made in 1970, this is a cult classic that's perfect for bachelor parties. First, there's very little plot. Second, there's plenty of intermittent nudity. Third, it's got a killer weird soundtrack. Fourth, have you ever seen a vampire lesbian horror film before?

Very Bad Things

A great cast (including Jon Favreau, Cameron Diaz, Jeremy Piven, and Christian Slater) experience bachelor party hell. They're in Las Vegas, the party stripper dies, they try to cover it up, and, of course, get into worse trouble. Comedy rarely gets darker than this.

Women in Cages

Pam Grier, the busty blaxploitation bimbo, is a mean prison guard who whips some of her all-female inmates and has sex with others. Surprisingly, there's a real plot here, too, which involves shady heroin dealers and prostitutes, but bachelor party viewers will most appreciate Grier's dungeon scenes.

WEIRD/SPECIALTY VIDEOS

For classic vintage stag films (1914–1969), peepshow loops, European loops (1970s–1980s), pinups and nudes (1920s–1980s) consider these sources:

www.alphabluearchives.com
www.bluevanities.com
www.eroticmedia.com
www.forbiddenfile.com

www.hotweird.com
www.mondofausto.com
www.somethingweird.com

Gags, Novelties, and Props

Even a highbrow evening discussing, say, the various regions of Australian wine country can benefit from the unexpected gag prop—party favors, poker cards, piñatas—to lighten the mood when dullness creeps in. Recognizing the need for all things boobalicious, manufacturers have molded faux breasts into every imaginable knickknack—from magnets to mugs.

Sometimes it seems like there are more Web sites and stores selling breast lollipops than there are customers. Still, these items are often inexpensive and could become valuable accessories should a stripper decide to get creative. Props are also great for scavenger hunts. At some bachelor parties, the men are divided into teams and set loose to find a laundry list of odd and embarrassing items, which may include:

- Blow-up dolls and blow-up sheep
- Condom hats, condom key chains, condom costumes, and flavored condoms

celebrity trivia: According to E! Online's gossip hound Ted Casablanca, actor-director Albert Brooks asked every guest at his bachelor party to bring three things: (1) a good book, (2) a really bad porn movie, (3) $10.

- Penis pumps—small and large
- Boob whistles, key chains, lollipops, water guns, candles, mugs, shot glasses, bottle stoppers, ice trays, straws, erasers, magnets, fishing lure, golf tees, and pasta
- Nudie cards (great for poker)
- Pin the Boobs on the Babe game
- Mistletoe with condom
- Glow in the dark back-scratcher with a naked woman handle
- Vagina-shaped soap on a rope

X-Rated Gag and Prop Web Sites

www.ebay.com (specifically: Home > All Categories > Everything Else > Gifts & Occasions > Gag Gifts, Novelties > Risqué Novelties)
www.adultgiftbaskets.com
www.nawtythings.com/novelties/bachlor.html

Erotic Cakes and Candies

Naughty cakes, those shaped like breasts and genitalia, are nothing new. Back in the sixties, men at stag parties could chomp on, say, a chocolate boob for a naughty giggle. But with the Internet boom and the ever-increasing threshold for shock value, men are demanding more erotic cakes with ever more explicit scenarios.

One New York City store, Mastur Bakers (212-475-0476), created a cake with a pregnant woman giving birth and another with a gorilla coming on a woman's face. Believe it or not, they put that one in the catalog and people have been ordering it ever since. Companies like these can turn batter and butter cream frosting into any body part—usually for between $40 and $100. One

Bachelor Joke

Three young men got together after a big bachelor party and were talking about how drunk they got the night before. The first guy said, "Man, I was so drunk last night I went home and blew chunks." The second guy said, "Man, that was nothing. I was so drunk last night I was driving home and I got a DWI." The third guy says, "Man, that was nothing. I was so drunk last night I was driving home and I picked up a prostitute and my wife caught us in bed." Then the first guy said, "No—you guys don't understand! Chunks is my dog!"

notable favorite is the cake shaped like a bottle of Budweiser—with the addition of female anatomy.

In Seattle, the Erotic Bakery (206-545-6969) also works with custom designs, but goes one step farther: They reproduce sexy photos on cakes. Hand over a snapshot of the groom and the Erotic Bakery will scan, digitize, and draw whatever you like on a cake. The bakery has done everything from she-male cakes to pinup girls to a naked belly dancer with a hatchet in her head and one eye dangling. For Vegas-style bachelor party planners, there's always the cake shaped like a slot machine with three vaginas across the windows and chocolate boobs falling out of the money slot.

Some bachelors believe that cake, in any shape, is too traditional (and you can't take it with you). That's why bakers also sell erotic snacks, like the sometimes-customizable lollipops, chocolate bars, cupcakes, and chocolate handcuffs. Sexworld Cakes (612-672-0556), for example, will ship custom orders twenty-four hours a day from their Minneapolis shop to anywhere in the United States. With five days advance notice, you can drop $29.95 for a dozen cupcakes. Or pay $39.95 for a small cake and $69.95 for a larger one and feed anywhere from fifteen to forty hungry mouths. Like many erotic bakeries, Sexworld also has a Web site (see guide below) with photos that display the bakers' goods.

Another shop, Sweet-N-Nasty (617-266-7171), won't ship actual cakes, but this Boston-based store will ship hundreds of naughty designs of adult candies. Titty Pops, the perfect treats to hand out to the guys before or after a beer, are available in chocolate and vanilla. Got leftovers? Make 'em party favors. Look for these and other garish goodies in the site's Daring Chocolate department.

What's especially nice about all these edible erotic options is that grooms don't have to hide the party details from their brides. Of course, you could always hire a stripper and slather her body with cherry sauce from the cake, but that's another story. . . .

celebrity trivia: Kitten Natividad, the mega-busty star of many a Russ Meyer film, danced at Sean Penn's bachelor party (when he wed Madonna) in 1985 at the Roxy Night Club on the Sunset Strip. When Harry Dean Stanton showed up late to the bash, according to Natividad's personal Web site, Penn picked up her blouse and said, "See what you missed?" and shoved Stanton's face into her cleavage.

Tasteless Bachelor Party Joke

QUESTION: Did you hear about the bulimic bachelor party?
ANSWER: The cake jumped out of the girl!

Erotic Baker Web Sites

www.chocolatefantasies.com
www.eroticchocolates.com
www.koppsbakery.com
www.naughtycakes.com
www.regalcakegallery.com
www.sexworld.com/Cakes/cakes.htm
www.sweet-n-nasty.com
www.theeroticbakery.com

Open-Container Laws

To drink or not to drink—especially in vehicles—that is the question. While most elbow bending is done in the home, tavern, or bleachers, there's an essential need to drink en route to any and all of those bachelor party destinations. And that's not always possible, legal, or safe. But even if you get someone else, maybe even a chauffeur, to drive as you imbibe, some pesky laws (which differ for each state) could potentially limit your fun.

Twenty-nine of the fifty states (plus Washington, D.C.) have "open container laws" as they pertain to alcoholic beverages in au-

> ## famous bachelor quote: Marriage is a great institution, but I'm not ready for an institution.
> —Mae West

tomotive vehicles, according to a chart obtained from the National Highway Traffic Safety Administration. What does that mean? According to the U.S. Department of Transportation, the open container law "prohibits the possession of any open alcoholic beverage container, or the consumption of any alcoholic beverage, in the passenger area of any motor vehicle (including possession or consumption by the driver of the vehicle) located on a public highway, or the right-of-way of a public highway, in the State."

Some states outlaw only the driver from drinking and some outlaw everyone in the vehicle from imbibing. Rhode Island is the most stringent, forbidding a person to "operate a motor vehicle upon the public highways with any unsealed alcoholic beverage container within the passenger section of said vehicle."

Boozing is allowed in limousines, however, because there is a glass partition that separates the driver from the passengers; the key element is that the driver cannot be in a position to handle any alcohol. Darting your body through the sunroof and swigging a bottle of champagne in plain view normally seems to be A-okay—provided you're not firing empties at elderly pedestrians. Folks in mobile homes can drink plenty too.

In almost all cases, walking—or stumbling, as the case may be—down the street with a bottle of Bud or a full brandy snifter is also against the law. Covering the Bud or bottle of bourbon with a brown paper bag doesn't make the wrong a right in most cases, either. In Las Vegas—the bachelor party capital of the U.S.—however, that's

Tales of Whoa: #10

Don't Try This at Home

I was very drunk even before my "friends" carried me into the Mitchell Brothers strip joint on O'Farrell Street. When I awoke from my stupor, a stripper was standing immediately in front of me pulling her ass cheeks apart. There were guys around me with flashlights trying to get a good angle on the sight. In my very inebriated state, I thought it'd be a good idea to insert my index finger into her anus. She squealed. *Then all hell broke loose.* Several very large men literally threw me in the air and onto a motorcycle outside—which collapsed. The owner of the bike was incensed both at me and at the bouncers. He was even madder when I threw up on the engine—he'd just parked, and the vomit made a hissing, popping sound as it slipped between the cooling fins. I don't remember getting home. My fiancée said she heard my friends dragging me up the stairs with my feet banging against each step. I remember staying in bed all next day.

—A friend of the author

acceptable. Here's a city that eagerly serves gamblers free alcohol expressly to impair their judgment, so it would be hypocritical to disallow boozehounds to transfer libations across the street.

"The city is supported by tourism, and if we're arresting tourists for walking from one hotel to another hotel holding a beer, there go our tourists," says Tirso Dominguez, a spokesman for the Las Vegas Metro Police. Las Vegas does have some element of decorum, however, and uses a "public nuisance law" to weed out the truly belligerent drunks. Those considered public nuisances are usually picked up for urinating, snoozing, or wandering around pants-free.

In New Orleans, walking and drinking booze is illegal, though rarely enforced as evidenced by the many, many Mardi Gras party tapes. "If there is a detriment to the safety of the public, those laws are enforced," says Lt. Marlon Defillo of the New Orleans Police Department, "but, naturally, we can't enforce all laws that are available." The penalties for drinking in public vary from state to state, city to city, and town to town, but all are always a misdemeanor and result in a fine of more than $500 and/or as many as ninety days in jail. (Although your lawyer would really have to suck to allow the latter consequence.)

tip: Some states may change their open container laws so as to avoid losing money that would otherwise go toward their highway construction. Does your state have an open container law? Ask your local precinct.

In some cases, the judge may play mommy dearest and demand you seek help for your "addiction." And repeat offenders may get a custom-made punishment. "There was an individual who was arrested dozens of times for public drunkenness and the judge got tired of that person coming into the court as a habitual offender," says Tim Maley, a patrol officer at the CHP headquarters in Sacramento. "[So he became] a ward of the court and he spent the rest of his days planting flowers in a custodial situation." That's a worst-case scenario.

Not to sound too motherly, but it's just plain stupid to risk arrest because you're afraid you'll lose your buzz in the five minutes it takes to get from the strip club to the after-hours party. Consider

> *trivia:* Baseball great Lenny Dykstra broke his collarbone in a car wreck after fellow ballplayer John Kruk's bachelor party.

the increased insurance rates, lawyer's fees, driver's license reissue fee, fines, and loss of revenue from your job after having to appear in court or be in jail, and we're talking upward of $10,000.

And you thought a hangover was the worst of your problems.

R-Rated Do's and Don'ts

Think of the suggestions below as the men's "rules," the short and simple and the quick and (quite) dirty.

- *Do*—Try to affect an air of bemused nonchalance if the naked woman who pops out of the cake turns out to be your sister.
- *Don't*—Bring cameras to the strip club unless you know they're allowed and you know you won't be capturing fuel for a breakup in the future.
- *Do* Appoint a designated speller who will remain sober and correctly spell the bride-to-be's name should tattooing become part of the evening's highlights.
- *Don't*—Use this particular occasion to confide in the groom that you have always wished that the two of you had explored an alternate sexual lifestyle together.
- *Do*—Remind out-of-state visitors of relevant local statutes involving intoxication, urination, public lewdness, and the appropriate discharge of firearms.

Tales of Whoa: #11

Growing Up Fast

I attended a bachelor party for a fifty-five-year-old guy who was marrying some thirty-year-old chick who looked like Cameron Diaz. There were about fifty Wall Street traders in a large hotel room—and most were much older than me. Everyone was snorting cocaine. Then these two strippers did their little show and said they were up for anything. It cost $100 per person to go to the bathroom for a blow job, and twenty men said, "Yes, please!" I didn't get one myself (no, really), but I coughed up a few bills for my friends—not just to be a good guy, but I figured I'd secure a better relationship with them, business-wise, in the future. Not to mention the blackmail potential (at least they would think of it that way). I never got a chance to take advantage of this, but I sure got more respect. I wasn't "the kid" anymore.

—Yet another friend of the author

Don't—End the evening by accidentally marrying the stripper.

Do—Pin your name and address inside your jacket. This will make it easier if later they have to identify your body.

Don't—Brawl. If you brawl here, what will you do at the reception?

FOUR
Hot Spots:
Las Vegas, Tijuana,
and New Orleans

Some towns are built for bachelor parties. These are cities of sin with dens of decadence, and increasingly, places where party-goers can choose to ignore or embrace the debauchery. While many exciting cities thrive across the country, three places stand out as bastions of bachelor party bravado. They are Las Vegas, Tijuana, and New Orleans.

Unlike New York and Los Angeles, these cities attract bachelor parties because they have highly concentrated areas of wine, women, and song. Vegas, for example, has "the Strip" and all of its amenities (bars, restaurants, casinos) in one place. New Orleans is party town, not just during Mardi Gras, but all year long thanks to Bourbon Street and a long tradition of general naughtiness. And Tijuana is near enough, exotic enough, cheap enough, and wicked enough to attract bachelors from all over.

So while you can find numerous strip clubs and bars in many cities, none provide the whole package quite like these three. I rounded up the best restaurants, bars, nightclubs, and alternative (PG-rated) activities I could find. I didn't look for bargains or secret hideaways so much as reputations for greatness. It's up to you to find the best combination of sights and sounds for your party (see the PG-rated section "Steak (and Cigars)" on page 85 for a list of the top-rated steakhouses across the U.S.A). Happy hunting.

Las Vegas, Nevada

Vegas is bachelor party Mecca. It's got everything you could want: desert heat, gorgeous girls, infamous landmarks, hotels, casinos, and a bunch of other attractions that have only recently received attention, including great bars, restaurants, outdoor activities (hiking, biking, golf), and museums. Start with a great meal. You have no excuse not to.

UPSCALE RESTAURANTS

If you're looking for a bargain, look elsewhere. This restaurant guide is for the men who want a great gourmet meal—admittedly, at a price. Think $100 a person bare minimum.

Andre's
European charm mixes with a great wine list at this French institution. Two locations.
> 401 South Sixth Street (between Las Vegas Boulevard and Seventh Street)
> 702-385-5016
> 3770 Las Vegas Boulevard South (between Harmon and Tropicana Avenues)
> 702-798-7151

Aqua
Seafood San Francisco–style at the Bellagio.
> 3600 Las Vegas Boulevard South (Flamingo Road)
> 702-693-7111

Aureole

You can opt to eat at Swan Court, overlooking the lake at this "progressive American" restaurant in the Mandalay Bay, created by chef Charlie Palmer.

  3950 Las Vegas Boulevard South (Hacienda Avenue)

  702-632-7401

China Grill

Trendy Asian-inspired fare with a dance club on Wednesday evenings.

  Mandalay Bay

  3950 Las Vegas Boulevard South

  702-632-7404

Chinois

Wolfgang Puck cooks up California-by-way-of-Asia-and-France cuisine in a prime location.

  Forum Shops at Caesar's Palace

  3570 Las Vegas Boulevard

  702-737-9700

Emeril's New Orleans Fish House

You either love or hate this celebrity chef, who "kicks it up a notch" here at the MGM Grand.

  3799 Las Vegas Boulevard South (Tropicana Avenue)

  702-891-7374

Le Cirque

The Bellagio's version is every bit as good as the New York original— but you have to like French food and wearing a jacket and tie.

  3600 Las Vegas Boulevard South (Flamingo Road)

  702-693-8100

Lutèce

A classic, classy French restaurant reborn at the Venetian Hotel.
  3355 Las Vegas Boulevard South (between Flamingo and
    Spring Mountain Roads)
  702-414-2220

Nob Hill

From the folks who brought you Aqua comes this nouveau American/
seafood eatery at the MGM Grand.
  3799 Las Vegas Boulevard South (Tropicana Boulevard)
  702-891-1111

Nobu

Legendary Japanese food—sushi—though portions can be small and
pricey.
  4455 Paradise Road (between Flamingo Road and Harmon
    Avenue)
  702-693-5090

Picasso

Beautiful decor and service from the man behind San Francisco's leg-
endary French restaurant Masa.
  3600 Las Vegas Boulevard South (Flamingo Road)
  702-693-7223

Piero's

Great Italian food in a place, off the strip, that feels like Old Vegas.
  355 Convention Center Drive (between Debbie Reynolds
    Drive and Paradise Road)
  702-369-2305

Postrio

Wolfgang Puck, again, re-creates masterpiece meals—this time a restaurant made famous in San Francisco.

    3355 Las Vegas Boulevard South (between Flamingo and
        Spring Mountain Roads)

    702-796-1110

Renoir

Top-notch French food—at a price.

    3400 Las Vegas Boulevard South (Spring Mountain Road)

    702-791-7353

Rosemary's Restaurant

Former executive chef for Emeril does continental cuisine right.

    8125 West Sahara Avenue (between Buffalo Drive and
        Cimarron Road)

    702-869-2251

Spago

Wolfgang Puck (again?!) serves up gourmet pizza at Caesar's.

    3500 Las Vegas Boulevard South (Flamingo Road)

    702-369-0360

Top of the World

New French-American cuisine with a great view.

    2000 Las Vegas Boulevard South (north of Sahara Avenue)

    702-380-7711

Wild Sage Café

American fare, off the strip, from Wolfgang Puck prodigies.

    600 East Warm Springs Road (Amigo Street)

    702-944-7243

STRIP CLUBS

These are among the best strip clubs in Vegas. Note: The policies concerning cover fees and drink minimums change all the
time, so they are not listed here. Try to get passes from a concierge
or cabbie.

Cheetah's

*You'll find beautiful topless dancers at this straightforward, classic
club.*

2112 Western Avenue

702-384-0074

Club Paradise

*The classiest topless joint in Vegas also offers fine dining and cigars,
but you'll pay for the luxuries.*

4416 Paradise Road

702-734-7990

Crazy Horse Too

*In keeping with the Greco-Roman design, the interior features a huge
stage and "Emperor's Room" (VIP lounge). Cute topless dancers, too.*

2476 South Industrial Road

702-382-8003

Deja Vu Showgirls

*The dancers are top-notch and nude, but the waitresses may try to
get you to "buy the lady" a drink one too many times—albeit nonalcoholic ones.*

3247 Industrial Road

702-894-4167

Little Darlings

Part of the Deja Vu chain, this club boasts nude dancing, private booths, a shower dance area, and themed fantasy rooms. But, alas, no booze.

1514 Western Avenue

702-366-1633

Olympic Garden Cabaret

A huge place with some of the finest topless gals in Vegas, this club always has loads of strippers to ogle at any time and highly respected lap dancers.

1531 South Las Vegas Boulevard

702-385-8987

The Palomino Club

Somehow, this became the only club in Vegas to offer nude dancers and alcohol. To get a dance from a lady onstage, just ask the maître d'.

1848 North Las Vegas Boulevard

702-642-2984

Spearmint Rhino

A good topless club with lots of food options, but reportedly not always enough chairs.

3344 Highland Drive

702-796-3600

Strip Tease

No, it has nothing to do with Demi Moore's movie. Yes, there's nude dancing. No alcohol.

3750 South Valley View Boulevard

702-253-1555

BROTHELS

For a list of brothels organized by area and including addresses and phone numbers, see the "Brothels" section, especially page 172.

TOPLESS REVUES

All of the better hotels have what they consider to be high-class sex shows (also known as cabaret shows). Most of these include nudity but it's very tame stuff. At the time of this writing the following shows were still playing (some play for years):

SHOW	HOTEL	NOTES	COST
La Femme	MGM Grand	Lots of dancing, great light shows, suitable for all audiences. Very fit, natural bodies, not the silicone sirens you might otherwise expect.	$50–$60
Folies Bergere	Tropicana	A replica of the show that was all the rage in Paris circa 1869, this show is now the longest-running such show in the United States. Look for beautiful showgirls to do the cancan, in addition to fabulous dancing, acrobats, costumes, and scenery.	$45–$55

SHOW	HOTEL	NOTES	COST
Crazy Girls	Riviera	This show was virtually made for bachelor parties. The gals are famous for two things: great asses and sexy costumes (see-through leotards, negligees, and leather chaps). Lots of g-strings and one nude scene.	$25–$35
Skintight	Harrah's	Leather, lace, feathers, and a few serious hotties, namely Miss Nude World Vanna Lace and *Playboy*'s "Wet and Wild" Shannon O'Keefe. Bonus: Every member of the cast sets foot out into the audience.	$40–$65 (includes dinner)
Jubilee	Bally's	Gigantic headdresses adorn the 74 or so fancy showgirls in this topless show. Bob Mackie helped with the costumes, which gives you an idea who this show is aimed at (think: fashionistas).	$50–$60
Midnight Fantasy	Luxor	A classy topless revue (yes it is possible), where each dancer takes a turn introducing her favorite kind of seduction. Egyptian outfits slowly fade to thongs.	$30

THE OTHER SIDE OF VEGAS

In the beginning, Las Vegas was a barren desert. No one lived there and no one had fun there. Then a bunch of lawless rebels started building casinos, and it became the international gambling capital—and a magnet for debauchery. Hotels started to make a lot of money and, like the crazed bettor with a hot hand, each threw down a lot more cash to lure a new type of clientele: families. While Vegas is now a desert Disneyland, it's still got some old-school character. You just have to look for it.

For bachelors and other party-goers, this means you can do far more than just place a wager, chow for cheap, and watch naked women. Here are ten activities that show the other sides of Vegas, organized into categories for ten personality types: punks, drunks, hikers/bikers, golfers, gamers, skydivers, seafarers, roller coaster riders, museum-goers, and retro swingers.

Punks

The scene: Double Down Saloon. Hidden dive, beat-up chairs, stained pool tables, leather jackets and combat boots; witness real, live drunken brawls!

The music: Black Flag, Pussy Galore, NOFX

The drinks: ass juice (the house drink—a mix of various spirits and fruit juices), tequila shots

The reason: cheap beer and even cheaper women

Cons: You came to Vegas for this?

Location:

Double Down Saloon

4640 Paradise Road

702-791-5775

Drunks

The scene: Downtown Las Vegas. Cheap hotels, 50-cent hot
   dogs, and a 50-foot-tall leprechaun (aka Mr. O'Lucky)

The music: Engelbert Humperdinck and Tom Jones

The drinks: 75-cent beers

The reason: easy walk from casino to casino, 2-dollar tables, a
   whiff of the seventies

Cons: slumming is slumming, no matter where you go

Location:

Fitzgerald's Casino

301 Fremont Street

702-388-2400 or

800-274-5825

Hikers/Bikers

The scene: Red Rock Canyon National Conservation Area.
   The great outdoors, blue skies, T-shirts, and shorts

The music: birds chirping, silence

The drinks: water, lots of it

The reason: hiking, biking, and mountain climbing make for
   a more natural high than winning big at craps

Cons: you'll sweat like you've never sweated before

Location:

Red Rock Canyon

20 miles west of Las Vegas.

Drive west (10 to 18 miles) on Charleston Boulevard (State
   Route 159), turn right into Red Rock Canyon

Golfers

The scene: Shadow Creek Golf Club at Mirage Resorts—18
   holes, plaid pants, visors or Kangol caps

The music: Bing Crosby, 101 Strings, easy listening

The drinks: gin and tonics, Scotch on the rocks

The reason: you wanna stay fit—yeah, right

Cons: see what you'll look like after forty years of marriage; also, hot hot hot out there on the course

Location:

Shadow Creek Golf Club

3 Shadow Creek Drive

702-399-7111

888-778-3387

Gamers

The scene: Game Works. Multilevel arcade/video playland, pimply teens, flashing lights

The music: modern rock, pop

The drinks: wine, beer, classic and exotic drinks

The reason: play old-school arcade games and pinball or newfangled high-tech rides

Cons: not for claustrophobics; and those games add up

Location:

Gameworks

3785 Las Vegas Boulevard South #10

702-432-4263

Skydivers

The scene: the sky—you falling from it at 120 mph

The music: Skychurch, Propellerheads, Air

The drinks: probably not a good idea

The reason: get a custom video of you and your buddies skydiving

Cons: nausea, vertigo

Location:
Vegas Extreme Skydiving
Twenty minutes south of the Las Vegas Strip
866-269-8687

Seafarers

The scene: Lake Mead cruise ship, Saturday afternoon, sunglasses and Docksiders

The music: samba, bossa nova, Latin

The drinks: Mexican beer . . . Bohemia or Corona

The reason: willingly or not, someone's going to get wet

Cons: the water smells like a sewer (it is one), is infested with kids, and temperatures could hit 125 degrees

Location:
Lake Mead Cruises

Take 93/95 (Highway 515) south from any major access road to the second stoplight in Boulder City (approximately 18 miles from Tropicana freeway entrance). Turn left at the stoplight and continue approximately 4 miles on Highway 93 toward Hoover Dam. Turn left onto Lakeshore Road (Highway 166). The entrance is approximately 3.5 miles down the road, on your right.

702-293-6180

Roller Coaster Riders

The scene: roller coasters—17 of them throughout Vegas

The music: screaming passengers and wind in your face at 80 mph

The drinks: don't even think about it

The reason: Soar 160 feet in 2.5 seconds (on the Big Shot) or hang 50 feet from the ground (on the Inverter)

Cons: you have to trek from casino to casino
Location:
Various hotels on and off the Strip including Manhattan
    Express (at New York, NY); Speed, The Ride (at the
    Sahara); and the Lighting Bolt (at the MGM)

Museum-Goers
The scene: Liberace Museum, Elvis-A-Rama Museum,
    Madame Tussaud's, The Guggenheim
The music: take a guess
The drinks: hide a flask
The reason: it's daytime entertainment—and you might learn
    something—plus, tickets are just $7.00 to $15 a head—
    about $90 less than those bombastic hotel magic shows,
    and a few grand less than a bad run of luck at the tables
Cons: what, is this an educational bachelor party?
Location:
Liberace Museum and Foundation
1775 East Tropicana Avenue
702-798-5595

Elvis-A-Rama Museum and Gift Shop
3401 Industrial Road
702-309-7200

Madame Tussaud's
3377 Las Vegas Boulevard South
702-642-6440

The Guggenheim
The Venetian
3355 Las Vegas Boulevard South
702-414-2440

Retro Swingers

The scene: Peppermill Inn (aka Fireside Lounge), seventies-era decor, lots of mirrors, fireplace, velvet interior

The music: Frank Sinatra, maybe some country tunes

The drinks: Scorpions or Mai Tais served in giant glasses with lots of fruit

The reason: it's like stepping into *Casino* with De Niro—actually, they really filmed that here

Cons: Pregnant waitresses also from seventies era

Location:

Peppermill Inn

2985 Las Vegas Boulevard South

702-735-4177

Tijuana, Mexico

Tijuana is just fifteen minutes from downtown San Diego, which makes it an ideal destination for bachelor parties—especially if the guys want bargain bawdiness. But this is a dangerous place, especially in the infamous red light district. Mexico is a Third World country where not everyone speaks English and where certain kinds of innocent people are targeted by both criminals and cops. That means you may be asked to hand over your money (U.S. cash works just fine) if you're not careful.

Lucky for you, a few businesses have sprung up to hold your hand during the trip. One former cabdriver in San Diego started a company called "TJ Nights" (619-200-9316) that now picks up parties in the San Diego city area and taxies them into Tijuana's red light district. The trip can include any and all of the following: visits to "adult erotic" destinations, meals, booze, and even more salacious activities. ("Prostitution is not legal, but we could work something out," admitted one company spokesman.) They provide transportation (so you drink all night), they talk to the locals, they deal with corrupt cops (yes, it has happened), and they bring you back to the U.S.A. The evening starts any time and ends whenever you like too. The company accommodates parties of eight to twenty men at $75 and up per person. Suggested photo op: Groom with sombrero, groom with donkey, groom with many many empty Mexican beer bottles (or eating the worm).

Final note: It's not just about boob bars, brothels, and burritos in Tijuana. A well-designed bachelor party might consider watching a greyhound race, a jai alai game, or a bullfight before embarking on cheap eats and booze.

Some rules apply:

- Be cautious.
- Don't be belligerent anywhere, anytime.
- Don't flash expensive jewelry.
- Get used to seeing beggars, especially children.
- Carry U.S. cash—you'll get better deals.
- For overnights, stick with hotel/motels in the good ole U.S.A.—National City, Chula Vista, San Ysidro, or San Diego—not the ones in Mexico. This will save you both money and peace of mind.
- Bring ID of some sort. U.S. citizens can enter Mexico for seventy-two hours or less without a passport or visa, but you ought to be able to prove your citizenship.
- Order drinks without ice—a good idea anywhere in Mexico.

tip: Calls to Tijuana from the U.S.A. require this prefix: 011-52-6646.

NIGHTCLUBS

You don't want to amble aimlessly at night, drunk, in TJ. Head to the Zona Rio area or specifically to nearby Avenida Revolucion (the tourist zone) for clubs and bars. The avenue is usually closed off to traffic at night, allowing pedestrians and party-goers to walk without fear of oncoming traffic. Some of these clubs are huge, some are tiny. Some attract mostly locals; others get their fair share of tourists. The more attractive the crowd, the more likely there will be a velvet rope, a bouncer, and a line outside to get in. Consider employing a company like TJ Nights to help you get in, especially if you have a party of fifteen drunk, touristy men.

Rodeo Santa Fe
The Wild West theme comes to life here thanks to a live indoor rodeo at midnight, a mechanical bull, and old-school cowboy (vaquero) *hats at this enormous, three-level club. Come early or else brave the crowds, especially on weekends. Look for the glowing purple and gold icicles on the roof. For country music fans and others who groove on the country vibe.*

In the Pueblo Amigo shopping center on Avenue Paseo,
   Zona Rio
(011-52-6646) 82-4967

Baby Rock
Popular disco with "shooter girls" (women who carry liquor bottles in holsters, ready to pour a shot down your throat) and lots of special effects.

Boulevard Paseo de los Héroes and Avenue Rio Tijuana,
   Zona Rio
(011-52-6646) 34-2404

Tangaloo

This is one of the newest clubs in town, with a great-looking clientele and posh interior—thus it's not always easy to get in. The Spanish Web site (www.tangaloo.com) offers a peek into the schedule of events and general club flavor.

3215 Avenue Monterrey

Fracc. Neidhart

(011-52-6646) 81-8091

GREYHOUND RACES

Like horse racing, only with greyhounds.

3 Hipodromo Caliente

Agua Caliente Boulevard at Tapachula 12027, downtown

(011-52-6646) 81-7811

JAI ALAI

Watch insane jai alai players hurl balls harder than rocks at a wall and catch the rebounds. You can bet on the action too, but it's hard to imagine how you'd do well unless you follow the sport regularly.

1100 Avenue Revolucion (at Calle 8)

(011-52-6646) 85-2524/*www.geocities.com/Colosseum /Sideline/7480/*

BULLFIGHTS

Not for the weak of stomach, Mexican bullfights—at least the last ones I have seen—can be brutal. Men on horses tire the bull by circling him and prodding him with spears. When the matador comes out, the bull is very angry, but getting exhausted. When the bull's head drops enough from fatigue, the matador delivers the deathblow. Bullfights are held every other Sunday between May and October in the El Toreo arena (sometimes held in the arena by the ocean). Tickets start at $11 (U.S.) for the cheap seats and go to over $40 for a view closer to the action.

Boulevard Agua Caliente, between Avenue Cuauhtemoc and
  Avenue Diego Rivera
(011-52-6646) 86-15-10

RESTAURANTS

Restaurants in Tijuana run the gamut from seedy dives to luxurious mansions with lots of variations in between. Don't be surprised to run into odd cuisines either: Persian, Japanese, Italian, and other specialties. Heed these warnings too:

- At some restaurants, no one speaks English and the menu may be in Spanish. Bring a translator or dictionary or pick another place.
- Many restaurants seem to think that loud music—often a live band—will delight customers. Not so: sometimes you can't hear anything, so find out in advance what to expect.
- Some restaurants will automatically add a tip to the bill— especially for large parties. Do not let this offend you. But do take note.

Cien Años
Perhaps the best gourmet Mexican restaurant boasts exotic food (manta ray burritos), great steaks, fine wine, and is across the street from bumper boats.

1407 José Maria Velazco
(011-52-6646) 34-3039

Cyrus

Feeling daring? Try the Persian food at this luxurious restaurant, though I doubt you've ever seen these exotic dishes before (Kashk-e-bademjan *anyone?*).

Escuadrón Zol Zona Rio

(011-52-6646) 201-3110

La Lena

This nineteen-year-old steakhouse has a panoramic view of one of the region's oldest golf courses, the Tijuana Country Club.

11191 Agua Caliente Boulevard

(011-52-6646) 86-4752

Mariscos Don Pepe

Best seafood in town, some say.

688 Fundadores Boulevard

(011-52-6646) 84-9086

Rivoli Brasiere—Hotel Lucerna

Continental cuisine, a little more expensive than some other places.

Paseo de Los Héroes at Rodriguez

(011-52-6646) 33-3900

Saverio's

Elegant Italian food, a tad pricey.

#207 Boulevard Sanchez Taboada esq. Escuadrón

(011-52-6646) 86-6502

New Orleans, Louisiana

You don't have to visit New Orleans during Mardi Gras to grab an eyeful—and earful and mouthful. The French Quarter is always humming with hot girls, hot jazz, and hot Cajun food. This is an old town with a spooky, sexy old vibe. Walk down the narrow streets and you'll find bars, clubs, and restaurants for all types: sports bars, blues bars, gentlemen's clubs, and people-watching places. In fact, the balcony bars alone offer a good setting for a bachelor party—babes bear breasts on Bourbon Street every weekend nowadays. If you do decide to visit during Mardi Gras, be prepared for crowds like you've never seen, and inflated prices to boot; it can easily cost $100 per person just to secure a great viewing spot.

As you might expect, the city offers more than just babes and booze. You can ride on a riverboat, take a swamp tour, eat at great restaurants, gamble on a floating casino, bowl in style, or rent a streetcar.

CASINOS

Bally's Casino New Orleans
You don't have to go to Vegas for gambling. Located on Lake Pontchartrain is a floating casino with slot machines, video poker, blackjack, mini craps, poker, and roulette.
   800-57-BALLY

Harrah's
Located in the French quarter, this 115,000-square-foot casino offers more than 100 tables (including blackjack, craps, baccarat, and live poker) and slot denominations from 1 cent to $500—2,900 slot machines in total.
   800-eHARRAH

HIPSTER BOWLING

New Orleans is known as the birthplace of more than just jazz these days; it's the home of rock and bowl, too. Where else can you listen to live rockabilly, blues, or swing while bowling . . . and get Zydeco dance lessons? At Mid-City Lanes (504-482-3133/*www. rockandbowl.com*), you'll party in an eighteen-lane bowling alley that sports an authentic 1958 look and feel.

Group parties are available for between $10 and $25 per person. The highest-end choice, "Option 5" on the Web site, is outlined as follows: "2 and ½ hours of bowling, bowling shoe rental, open bar: premium brand liquors, bottled domestic beers & imported beers, draft beers, wine, fountain soft drinks. Vegetable tray and party sandwiches included." Plus food, which includes choice from a menu including jambalaya, shrimp pasta, crawfish and andouille pasta, red beans and rice, chicken Creole, Louisiana lasagna, pepperoni pizza tray, buffalo wings tray, fried seafood tray, and more. Hell, I'd go for the food alone.

RENT A STREETCAR

Who knew you could rent a streetcar (aka a trolley) for $200 and bring fifty of your closest friends? The streetcar travels approximately eight miles in total and takes about an hour and a half—only one loop unless you want to rent it again. If you're lucky enough to get a good conductor, you can encourage him to make occasional stops (don't forget to tip). For music, bring a boom box. For food and drink, bring your own. And if you have extra cash, hire a brass or jazz band—they may even play for food and drink. Along the way, you can see some of the great old homes on Carrollton and St. Charles. Bring a camera to take some good pictures of the gawkers, which surely will include cutie-pie tourists.

You might as well bring some Mardi Gras beads, too. Avoid throwing beads to the locals; they get enough of them during other parades. A few words to the wise: Don't throw trash out the window, don't hang out of the streetcar windows (telephone poles are very close to the tracks), don't ask if you can drive, and, finally, don't ask the conductor to floor it. He probably already is going top speed. Call the regional transit authority at 504-940-3146 for more info (two-week advance notice required). Photo or video ops: on the trolley with buddies or invite the hotties on the street into the car for a while.

Gentlemen's Clubs

Bourbon Street is stripper central, so you can stroll and duck inside as many clubs as you like, anytime you like.

Temptations Club

One of the city's favorite clubs offers catering, open bar, prepurchased kegs and champagne, entertainers, balconies to Bourbon Street, billiards, bachelor party cakes, videotaping, and photographs. Private VIP suites are available per hour. You can even contact the club's personal party planner at 504-522-1925.

327 Bourbon Street

504-525-4470

www.temptationsclub.net or

www.temptationsneworleans.com

Big Daddy's

522 Bourbon Street

504-581-7167

Bourbon Burlesque Club
327 Bourbon Street
504-561-8057

Can Can Cabaret
300 Bourbon Street
504-524-9076

RESTAURANTS

Since most bachelor parties will swarm to the French Quarter, I've listed the best restaurants in this part of town only. God knows there's enough to choose from.

Antoine's
Either you believe that this French Quarter, Creole/French restaurant is the perfect locale for a big party (it's got fifteen separate dining rooms) or you think it's a tourist trap. Maybe it's both. Built in 1840, it's certainly a landmark.
713 St. Louis Street (between Bourbon Street and Royal
     Street)
504-581-4422

Dickie Brennan's Steakhouse
The classy, dark-wood environment sets the mood for carnivores who devour the stupendous filet mignon with fried oysters. Not cheap but worth every penny.
716 Iberville Street (Royal Street)
504-522-2467

Galatoire's

Great atmosphere and friendly waiters make this a true New Orleans experience.

209 Bourbon Street (Iberville Street)

504-525-2021

GW Fins

Newish. Upscale seafood—including superb fried lobster tail and scallops—in a recently renovated warehouse space.

808 Bienville Avenue (between Bourbon Street and
    Dauphine Street)

504-581-3467

K-Paul's Louisiana Kitchen

Tourists flock to Paul Prudhomme's place for blackened anything—though it's pricey and often filled to capacity.

416 Chartres Street (between Conti Street and St. Louis Street)

504-524-7394

Louis XV

The place is elegant though the servers are oddly standoffish at this classic French favorite.

730 Bienville Avenue (between Bourbon Street and
    Royal Street)

504-581-7000

Pelican Club

Old Louisiana Creole meets Asian fusion in this often crowded club-like restaurant.

312 Exchange Place (Bienville Avenue)

504-523-1504

Peristyle

Fantastic French-American cuisine with a great wine list.

1041 Dumaine Street (North Rampart Street)

504-593-9535

Rib Room

Old faithful steakhouse still pleases all comers with fabulous Martinis to boot.

621 St. Louis Street (between Chartres Street and Royal Street)

504-529-7046

FIVE
Beyond the Bachelor Party

Bachelor Party Toasts

In some cases, especially roasts and dinners, it's a good idea for someone to toast the groom. This is a much shorter toast than the ones recited at weddings. And it can be as embarrassing or as lewd as you want. Below are some classic bachelor toasts.

1. "Drink, my buddies, drink with discerning / Wedlock's a lane where there is no turning / Never was owl more blind than lover / Drink and be merry, lads, and think it over."

2. "I'll toast the girls who do / I'll toast the girls who don't. / But not the girls who say they will / And later decide they won't. / But the girl I'll toast from break of day / To the wee hours of the night / Is the girl who says, 'I never have—but just for you, I might!'"

3. "May it never fail ya: your genitalia."

4. "Who is a friend but someone to toast, someone to gibe, someone to roast. My friends are the best friends: loyal, willing, and able. Now let's get to drinking—glasses off the table!"

*"Thank goodness there are still a few people
left who aren't anti-establishment."*

tip: Practice in front of a mirror first, so you can see how you look, what your hands are doing, and how the words sound when spoken aloud. Plus, you can time the speech/toast so you know how long it takes.

Groomsmen's Gift Guide

Wherever there's a bachelor party, there's also a wedding. And that means someone is picking a best man and groomsmen to deliver speeches and do the grunt work: ushering, formalwear coordination, handling last-minute problems. They'll be at the rehearsal dinner. They'll do the dirty work. They need to be rewarded.

Gift options are plentiful. Assume you'll spend around $50 per person. Strapped for cash? You can get away with $15 per person. Got money to burn? It's easy to spend $150 per person—you want silver, gold, platinum . . . engraved? Ask your salesperson if you get a discount for bulk purchases. Here are some common—and not so common—gift ideas. These may be presented to the fellas at the bachelor party or at a rehearsal dinner.

Traditional

- Tie clip
- Money clip
- Flask/bottle opener/barware
- Cuff links
- Swiss army knife/pocket tools
- Cigar accessories (lighter or cutter)

- Binoculars
- Fancy pen
- Watch
- Leather wallet

Nontraditional

- Sports equipment (football, basketball, skates, etc.)
- Tickets to a big upcoming game
- Good bottle of Scotch or wine
- Subscription to *Playboy*
- Digital/Polaroid camera
- One hour with a professional masseuse
- Gag gifts (magic tricks, blow-up dolls, customized or sterling silver yo-yos, water guns, and so on)
- Gift certificates (sports stores, record stores, Beef-Jerky-of-the-Month Club, etc.)

"Reverse" Bachelor Parties (aka Divorce Parties)

If you think about it, the bachelor party comes at the wrong time in life. Why would a man who's just spent twenty, thirty, forty

---

celebrity trivia: Rumor has it that porn prince Matt Zane threw Korn's Jonathan Davis's bachelor party. The festivities included a she-male, a dominatrix, and some sort of intersection between a little skinny woman and a big fat woman and a double dong. Oh, and an eight-gal orgy with Davis in the center.

years of his life looking for love—and, finally, decided he's ready to give up the bachelor life and commit to one person—bring in a stripper now? Wouldn't it make more sense to throw a bachelor party when he's getting a divorce—when he's ready to be single (a bachelor) again?

That's the idea behind reverse bachelor parties, also known as divorce parties. Yes, this is basically a typical bachelor party, but there are far fewer concerns about do's and don'ts. No worrying about a fiancée, her family, the friends. In fact, at some such parties, the ex-groom burns the marriage license. Must have been a really bad marriage.

Most formerly married men have a better idea of what they really want—as in a PG- or R-rated party—than they did before their first marriage. What's more, older men often are further along professionally and so have more money to blow. Since there's no best man, it's up to one of three people to plan this party:

1. A friend—perhaps as a surprise
2. A relative—like a brother or uncle
3. The divorcé himself

Some companies are beginning to specialize in this form of entertainment. At Dick's Last Resort in Boston (617-267-8080/

---

famous bachelor quote: Bachelors have consciences, married men have wives.

—H. L. Mencken

> trivia: What was Tom Hanks's occupation in *Bachelor Party*? (Answer: school bus driver.) Who got the part before him but was axed one week into filming? (Answer: Paul Reiser.)

www.dickslastresort.com), they've perfected the craft. "Dick's Divorce Party" offers up food and cheer plus a few extras. The lucky divorcé is treated to "Break-Up Cake," a "Bobbitt Love Sundae," and an "Eraser Shot" topped with a condom that perks up when the glass is shaken. And you get to walk away with a brand-new little black book, a free personal ad, and a condom—all in the name of greener romantic pastures.

To Lie or Not to Lie: What to Tell the Bride Afterward

So it's the day after the big bachelor party and you had a great time: You don't remember a thing. Or maybe you had a terrible time and you remember everything. Either way, your girlfriend coyly asks, "So, how'd it go last night?" You panic. Do you tell the truth or build the bedrock of your relationship on a thin tissue of lies?

You know how risky this can be if you ever prodded and wheedled, bullied and begged your gal into telling you about her past love life only to be haunted forever by the image of her and that beast. You want to deck him, don't you?

Now imagine her reaction to even the slightest details from your bachelor night. Your fiancée may think she wants to know it

Tales of Whoa: #12

High School Reunion

About a dozen friends promised the groom a stripper with "a body that will make you cry." The woman, "Holly," was ushered from the door to the back bedroom to change. When she made her grand entrance in the living room, everybody's jaw dropped—especially the groom's. The stripper was not only gorgeous, but also his high school sweetheart. For a moment, both just stared at each other, uncertain what to do. After some private conversation, the former couple decided the show must go on, and she gave a performance to remember.

all, but she'll find it hard to forget the picture of your lips planted on anything other than a few pints of beer.

Hopefully she's been enjoying a steamy bachelorette night of her own and may not want to reveal how she stuffed a twenty down some male stripper's jock . . . with her teeth. But let's say you did go a little too far. Or she needs a little more reassurance; perhaps she's a trifle insecure, suspicious even. In that case, you need to be honest, calm, and composed. Or blame it all on your friends. Or lie like there's no tomorrow. No matter what you choose, you had better have gotten your story straight with all the other guys who attended the party since they, too, have girlfriends and wives who will want to know what the boys did. Here is a simple sample script that may help you get through this once-in-a-relationship dilemma:

WRONG WAY TO HANDLE IT

SHE: So what happened?

YOU: Nothing. We went out, had a few laughs . . . don't worry, okay?

Note: You're making her very worried by being vague. Try to include harmless details instead.

RIGHT WAY TO HANDLE IT

SHE: So what happened?

YOU: It was a bachelor party. There were a bunch of guys, I knew maybe half of them, we went to a restaurant, had dinner, went to a bar, and drank a lot. Most of us talked about our girlfriends . . .

Note: She'll want to know what you said about her—which immediately steers the conversation away from what you did and toward her. Explain how routine the night was. Focus on the details of the meal and drinks; what did you order? Tell her you would have had more fun spending the night with her instead. Hopefully, you mean it.

Maybe the groom not only did something a teensy-weensy bit immoral, but he's so overcome with guilt that he feels the need to

tip: If you fear that your girlfriend/wife will not understand (or believe) your explanation of what happened at this party, pick up some flowers for her on the way home. Then again, this might tip her off that something really bad happened. . . .

"What was that bit about forsaking all others?"

Tales of Whoa: #13

I Don't

A conservative groom, after much prodding, let his friends convince him to allow a stripper to come to the party. Several drinks into the evening, the groom wound up having sex with the stripper in another room. Everybody at the party knew what happened and also knew the groom felt horrible about it, but one man felt obligated to leak the news to the bride-to-be. The next day, the wedding day, the bride kept the news to herself all day—until she was at the altar. When the preacher asked if anybody had just cause why this couple should not be united, the bride raised her hand. "I know a reason, because this asshole fucked a stripper last night!" she said as she stormed off. According to reports, the couple eventually got married anyway, at a doubtlessly tense second wedding ceremony.

bare his soul and tell his wife-to-be about his shenanigans—instead of hiding it. This is certainly noble and honest. It is also dangerous.

Only the groom can decide what counts as a petty offense and what's a major blow (pardon the expression) to the relationship. For some men, nothing jeopardizes the wedding, period; many wives would argue the point. For other men, it's a hard call. Does it matter if the stripper kisses you on your bachelor party night? Probably not. How about if she performs a little oral gratification on you? Well, now that's a horse of a different color. And, frankly,

Tales of Whoa: #14

Proof Is in the Pudding

The groom-to-be swore to his fiancée that he wasn't going to engage in any shenanigans with the stripper (don't we all?). But then came the drinks, and the strip-tease, and the howling from his friends. After a while, he found himself alone in a dark hotel bedroom and in professional hands. The stripper went down on him and apparently did the condom trick (having a condom hidden in her mouth and slyly unrolling it a bit onto him while working away). When he returned home from the bachelor party, his fiancée was awake. As he explained how the bachelor party was just like any other get-together, no big deal, he got undressed and removed his pants to reveal . . . yes, the dangling and filled evidence.

brides-to-be are not eager to hear about moral shortcomings days before their wedding. Too much soul baring (truth telling) will only exacerbate an already tense situation. Now might be a good time to develop a story.

Remember: Explain what happened—but don't dwell on details this time. Blame your actions on 1) the aggressive stripper, 2) the endless booze, or 3) your goading friends. If it's true love, things will work out. If you know she'll dump you, well, only you can decide what's worth lying about.

How about if she confronts you because someone told her *exactly* what happened? Now, you have no choice but to invoke the blaming game (as described in paragraph above) and grovel. Get down on your knees. Force a few tears out. Use the "L" word. Apologize. Promise it will never happen again (it won't, right?). If you need extra leverage, try to explain how it happened, but focus on the remarkable strength you called up throughout the night, putting off this horrendous offense, until you were overcome with a wave of brash, foolish bravado. Tell her about the many many times you rebuffed advances by the stripper. Tell her about the

How to Remove Lipstick Stains

Busted. It's a word you don't want to hear the morning after. It doesn't matter if you merely endured a bad lap dance—or actually slept with the stripper. Lipstick traces on your shirt, suit, pants, and/or undies will get you into big trouble back at home.

The reason why lipstick does not just come out lickity-split, so to speak, is because it is oil-based and filled with dyes. So if you try to wash it with soap and water, not only will you set the stain, you will also spread it. Plenty of purported remedies line store shelves, but only two products completely remove stains. The first is DidiSeven, available at most stores for about $5.00 per two-ounce tube. *Consumer Reports* had deemed it the best stain remover. The only drawback is that it uses a rather harsh chemical, which could damage delicate garments. For more sensitive fabrics, try EverBlum Cosmetic Stain Remover. This product is harder to find, only available in fabric shops, but professional cleaners swear by it ($11 for eight ounces).

way you knew you loved her too much to hurt her in any way . . . and that you don't know how you slipped. It's a fog, a nightmare, an inexplicable lapse not only in judgment, but in character. That's right: Plead temporary insanity. It works in court, after all. My guess is that she wants to believe you.

COMBINING ACTIVITIES

You've perused all the activities in this book and found some worth considering. But a steak dinner alone does not a party make. So you're trying to figure out what group of activities works best together. I'll make it easy for you. Look at the chart below and combine any number of activities from columns A, B, and C. Your best bet is to grab a daytime activity from column A (golfing, fishing, etc.) with an early nighttime activity from column B (dinner, roast, etc.) and a late-night activity from column C (strip club, pub, disco, etc.). But you can also pair two items from column B with one from column C if there is no daytime activity. Or combine any number of activities, from any column, in any order you like.

Here's an example: If you want a retro dinner, you might start a Saturday with a round of golf, then retire to a good steakhouse for dinner, transition into a roast (with cigars), and end the night by having a stripper jump out of a cake and perform for you. The combinations are limitless. Just remember to pace yourself.

A (daytime)	B (early evening)	C (late-night)
Fishing	Steak Dinner	Strip Club
Golfing	Gambling	Stripper at Hotel
Camping/Hiking/Rafting	Roast	Stripper Jumps out of Cake
Paint Ball/Laser Tag	Scotch or Wine Tasting	Karaoke
Skydiving/Bungee Jumping	Bowling	Booze Cruise
Baseball Game	Poker	Pub Crawl
Skiing/Snowboarding	Arcade/ Amusement Park	Disco
Dude Ranch/Hunting		Drinking Games
Car Racing/Bumper Cars		Watch Videos
Massage/Spa		Bonfire
Gambling at the Horse Track		
Cruise		
Barbecue		
Scavenger Hunt		
Sports Tournaments		

Bachelor Party Planner's Checklist

Preliminary Planning:
Who, What, Where? When?

❏ Get wedding date from groom
❏ Ask groom what kind of party he wants
❏ Find out if there is a target budget
❏ Decide if cigars, limos, and beer or liquor should be procured
❏ Write down names and numbers of guests groom would like to invite
❏ Calculate total number of party attendees based on potential guest list

Making Reservations

❏ Research and then book hotel room, stripper, limo, etc.
❏ Pay all necessary deposits
❏ Calculate fee for each guest
❏ Come up with a Plan B, just in case

Inviting Guests

❏ Decide on how to invite bachelor party invitees: mail, e-mail, Web-based system, or phone
❏ Create a phone tree detailing who will call whom with party details
❏ Contact guests on the list and explain party date, time, location, costs, dress code, and fee

❑ Arrange a way for guests to RSVP easily: phone, e-mail, or Web-based invite system

❑ Arrange a way for guests to pay you immediately

Week Before Party

❑ Finalize log of RSVPs

❑ Call all companies and confirm reservations

❑ Practice toasts to the groom

❑ Purchase cigars, booze, mints, condoms, aspirin, bottle openers, cigar cutters

Day Before Party

❑ Print out names and phone numbers of all attendees

❑ Print out names and contacts of all businesses involved: limo, hotel, stripper, etc.

❑ Print out complete evening itinerary

❑ Prepare a kit filled with mints, condoms, aspirin, bottle openers, and cigar cutters

❑ Withdraw cash for party—including lots of singles for tips and strippers

Day of Party

❑ Call all guests only if you must resort to Plan B

❑ Show up at first destination thirty minutes early

❑ Bring cell phone, prep kit, itinerary, guest information, cigars, booze, and cash

❑ Collect guest fees

Day After Party

❑ Explain lipstick stains to girlfriend

❑ Continue to collect guest fees

❑ Check up on groom and make sure he is still getting married

❑ Sleep

INDEX

ACKNOWLEDGMENTS

Many people helped conceive, design, and edit this book. I would like to thank David Justus, who early on identified the need for a bachelor party guide. Jonathan Black, too, immediately recognized the value of such a guide and he has been consistently patient, encouraging, and helpful. Special thanks to Paula Balzer and Sarah Lazin, who held my hand throughout the book proposal process. Matt Walker, Jake Klisivitch, and Marcela Landres shaped the book with keen observations and a bevy of right-on-the-money questions.

During research, many people went beyond the call of duty to immerse me in their particular areas of bachelor party expertise. They include Lonnie Hanover, Dennis Hof, David Schlow, Adrian Morgan, Rob Tewlow, and Tim Lee. Special thanks go out to Michelle Urry, Jennifer Thiele, and Marcia Terrones for making the visuals happen.

Finally, I would like to thank my immediate family—Peter, Lynda, and Ivan Cury—for reading early drafts and telling me when I made no sense. Most important, I thank Dorothy Krasowska for not only reading the book over and over again, but for her relentless encouragement—and for the graceful nonchalance with which she answered the phone and unwittingly spoke to working girls, brothel owners, and other odd characters who inhabit the world of bachelor parties.

ABOUT THE AUTHOR

James Oliver Cury, former lifestyle editor at *Playboy.com,* is a regular contributor to *Playboy* magazine. He has also written for *Details, US, Entertainment Weekly, Cosmopolitan, Spin,* and *Time Out New York*. A graduate of Wesleyan University, he lives in New York City with his fiancée. A bachelor party is in the works.